WITHDRAWN

EXPERIENCING PROGRESSIVE ROCK

The Listener's Companion
Kenneth LaFave, Series Editor

Titles in **The Listener's Companion** provide readers with a deeper understanding of key musical genres and the work of major artists and composers. Aimed at nonspecialists, each volume explains in clear and accessible language how to *listen* to works from particular artists, composers, and genres. Looking at both the context in which the music first appeared and has since been heard, authors explore with readers the environments in which key musical works were written and performed.

EXPERIENCING PROGRESSIVE ROCK

A Listener's Companion

Robert G. H. Burns

ROWMAN & LITTLEFIELD
Lanham • Boulder • New York • London

Published by Rowman & Littlefield
An imprint of The Rowman & Littlefield Publishing Group, Inc.
4501 Forbes Boulevard, Suite 200, Lanham, Maryland 20706
www.rowman.com

Unit A, Whitacre Mews, 26-34 Stannary Street, London SE11 4AB

British Library Cataloguing in Publication Information Available

Library of Congress Cataloging-in-Publication Data

Names: Burns, Robert G. H. author.
Title: Experiencing progressive rock : a listener's companion / Robert G. H. Burns.
Description: Rowman & Littlefield, [2018] | Series: Listener's companion | Includes bibliographi-
    cal references and index.
Identifiers: LCCN 2017053260 (print) | LCCN 2017054077 (ebook) | ISBN 9781442266032 (elec-
    tronic) | ISBN 9781442266025 (cloth : alk. paper)
Subjects: LCSH: Progressive rock music—History and criticism
Classification: LCC ML3534 (ebook) | LCC ML3534 .B8636 2018 (print) | DDC 781.66—dc23
    LC record available at https://lccn.loc.gov/2017053260

♾ ™ The paper used in this publication meets the minimum requirements of
American National Standard for Information Sciences Permanence of Paper
for Printed Library Materials, ANSI/NISO Z39.48-1992.

Printed in the United States of America

CONTENTS

SERIES EDITOR'S FOREWORD

The goal of the Listener's Companion series is to give readers a deeper understanding of pivotal musical genres and the creative work of its iconic composers and performers. This is accomplished in an inclusive manner that does not necessitate extensive music training or elitist shoulder rubbing. Authors of the series place the reader in specific listening experiences in which the music is examined in its historical context with regard to both compositional and societal parameters. By positioning the reader in the real or supposed environment of the music's creation, the author provides for a deeper enjoyment and appreciation of the art form. Series authors, often drawing on their own expertise as both performers and scholars, deliver to readers a broad understanding of major musical genres and the achievements of artists within those genres as lived listening experiences.

No other musical genre is as loudly despised as the one that is the subject of this thoughtful, engaging book by Rob Burns. Burns goes some distance to explain why this is so, and if the skeptical reader at book's end is more inclined to listen to progressive rock without disdain, it's because he brings to this book his own background as a classical musician who immigrated to rock, adding critical insights and a grasp of the genre's difficult history.

The names of prog rock artists are as familiar as any other pop culture names, among them King Crimson, Jethro Tull, Procol Harum, Yes, Genesis, and Emerson, Lake and Palmer. But there hangs around them the air of something separate and apart from the mainstream.

Here is music that quotes Holst and Copland, references jazz, and uses progressions from Bach and Dvorak as harmonic frames. What did these groups think they were doing? Apparently they didn't get the memo from John Lennon: "Before Elvis, there was nothing."

There has always been an air of elitist purity around the critics who dismiss progressive rock. I recall a friend in college asking me, "What's your favorite rock group?" Answered I: "Emerson, Lake and Palmer." "That," my friend sniffed, "is not real rock." "Real rock" is that which has its roots no deeper than the 1950s. Only, how is that possible? Fifties rock 'n' roll came from rhythm and blues, which came from the blues, which in turn resulted from African Americans' encounters with Western music decades previous. No music genre lives alone. Music is a tree, every genre is a branch, and the roots run in every direction.

And yet, the anti-prog prejudice continues, at least in some quarters. Writer Kelefa Sanneh offered a thoughtful appreciation of the genre in the June 19, 2017, *New Yorker* magazine that, when casually read, seems a fair, even positive, appraisal. But a closer read reveals subtle dismissals. The genre's main appeal, writes Sanneh, was "not spiritual, but technical." Prog rock's creators were "rather nerdy." And part of the genre's very identity was its inherent "uncoolness." Sanneh is generally receptive to the value of prog rock but is forced by pop culture's judgments to heavily qualify his assessment.

Burns, by contrast, looks at the genre without prejudice to hear what the bands have to say. As noted earlier, readers of the Listener's Companion series should come away with a clearer grasp of why they feel the way they do about certain genres and pieces of music. This demands from the writer the ability to describe music in everyday terms, not in academic jargon. It also requires the writer to go deep using only these simple verbal tools.

Burns does this throughout, outlining a number of factors that made prog rock what it was. Varied instrumentation that moves well beyond guitars and drums, tending to favor the keyboard; a high level of technical mastery that echoes classical virtuosity; and most of all, perhaps, harmonic sophistication. In one insightful look at a key prog rock song, Burns examines "Machine Messiah" by Yes and lays out why it is effective. He's careful to include mention of the particular harmonic mode that shapes the song's basic sound and still more careful to explain how that mode sounds and why it is essential to the song's character.

Prog rock enjoyed a heyday in the 1970s and, as Burns and other critics have pointed out, it was brought down hard in the early 1980s by punk. Major prog rock bands retired or took a hiatus in the wake of punk's insistence that rock equals guitars and drums playing a basic beat and a few chords to a biting social commentary. But punk didn't uproot the tree of music and plant a new one; it added a graft. And although the graft initially outgrew the other branches, the others still remain today. Burns's book is testimony to the continued and renewed interest in the most hated—and secretly loved—genre in rock history.

Kenneth LaFave

ACKNOWLEDGMENTS

Thank you to my series editor and everyone at Rowman & Littlefield, principally Kenneth Lefave, Natalie Mandziuk, and Darren Williams, without whom I could not have completed this book.

I am also deeply indebted to my friends and colleagues in the music industry, most of whom were at the beginnings of progressive rock, and others who joined along the way. All have been willing to share memories and current experiences with me for the purposes of this book. I am grateful that all were open and frank in their personal descriptions of a musical style that has been through many changes during the last four decades and that has attracted criticism and praise from a variety of respected music critics. My informants include Jakko Jakszyk (King Crimson), Clem Clempson (Colosseum; Jack Bruce), Nick Beggs (John Paul Jones; Steven Wilson; Steve Hackett; the Mute Gods), John Knightsbridge (the Yardbirds; Third World; Illusion; and Renaissance), Gary O'Toole (Steve Hackett; China Crisis), David Glasser (Grammy award–winning mastering engineer), Tony Levin (King Crimson; Peter Gabriel; Paul Simon; the Liquid Tension Experiment; and many more), Rick Fenn (10cc; Rick Wakeman; David Gilmour), Paul Burgess (10cc; Camel; Jethro Tull), Terry Pack (the Enid), Robin Lumley (Phil Collins and Brand X), and Steven Wilson (composer, performer, producer, and founder of Porcupine Tree). Some have allowed me to write about our experiences as professional musicians since the 1970s, others still have given me interviews throughout 2016 and into 2017.

Equally, I have had the privilege and pleasure of working with some of the greatest performer/composers of the twentieth and twenty-first centuries; I am in your debt for developing my experience. From my first days as a professional musician, I must acknowledge bassist Roy Babbington, who took time to coach me as a young bassist when my band supported Soft Machine on a European tour in the mid-1970s. He provided many insights into the processes involved in improvisation. Thank you, Roy. I must also thank composer Howard Goodall, who appreciated my input to his wonderful music composed for television programs for two decades; thank you, Howard.

My appreciation goes on. Thank you to my friends and colleagues Ian Chapman, Andrew Deruchie, Graeme Downes, Roger Knott, and Trevor Coleman for being my advisers, as well as the technological wonder that is Sandi Jull, who performed the formatting of this work—another thank you.

I am lucky to have two sons, Jake and Alex, both excellent guitarists who have introduced me to several (post) progressive bands that have become part of my regular listening list.

Thank you, too, to Sue, who has become used to being asked to let me be a hermit.

Finally, my sincere thanks go to several musicians who have passed on in the last few years: Jon Lord, John Wetton, Greg Lake, Chris Squire, Keith Emerson, Allan Holdsworth, and John Entwistle. They were all inspirational, and those of them whom I knew personally during my musical career were always kind and encouraging.

INTRODUCTION

Although this book is not a definitive chronological history of progressive rock music from the perspective of all its progenitors and the albums they released, it does follow a broad chronological time line that initially draws upon the rich history of the style since its inception in the late 1960s before moving through its various stylistic and technological developments in the 1970s and 1980s and on to a progressive rock revival that was, to an extent, driven by baby boomer nostalgia during the 1990s and into the twenty-first century. At this point, progressive rock's focus in this book becomes more broad as the style became, at the time, accessed by a younger generation of musicians and curious music fans seeking music that was both challenging and different from the pop/rock styles of modern times. The contemporary revival has taken place at a time when 1970s bands either reunited (for example, the Moody Blues, Caravan, and Colosseum, with Van Der Graaf Generator reuniting in 2003 following a "one-off" reunion in 1996) or continued to enjoy success without having stopped performing, many in stadia contexts, in the way that they had enjoyed since the heyday of their first successes in the late 1960s and 1970s (for example, Pink Floyd, Yes, Marillion, the Who, and King Crimson—a band like several other progressive bands that took several breaks from recording and performance). It should be noted that there are now many new "progressive" bands that have formed since the late 1980s and remain influenced by those of the 1970s or have formed in the last two decades and continue to create new combinations or "fusions" that make the genre progress.

It is also worth noting that many early progressive rock bands had their origins in the 1960s but changed their styles following the growth of the counterculture on both sides of the Atlantic in the late 1960s. One must acknowledge the release of several seminal albums, some from the same London recording studios from 1967 onward, and it therefore could be argued that early progressive rock was Eurocentric in its orgins, given the amount of European classical music performed (although Emerson, Lake and Palmer recorded Aaron Copland's *Fanfare for the Common Man* in 1972). There were, however, many U.S. bands who took various American music styles and adapted them for contemporary performance; for example, the Byrds' folk-rock adaptation of Americana on *Sweetheart of the Rodeo* (1968); the rock-, jazz-, and funk-driven music of Chicago and Blood, Sweat and Tears; the experimental instrumentalism of Flock and It's a Beautiful Day; the fusion of traditional Latin music with rock and blues by Santana; the early extended compositions recorded by Los Angeles band Love (although, in this band's case, the line between earlier psychedelia and the later progressive rock is a fine one); and the groundbreaking fusion of rock and jazz and other styles in the Mahavishnu Orchestra, Return to Forever, and Weather Report. It would be even more difficult to describe Frank Zappa's prolific output from the psychedelia of the Mothers of Invention in the late 1960s and early 1970s to his complex compositions of the 1980s, which drew on a variety of styles from doo-wop harmony vocals to jazz and the influences he took from Edgar Varese (1883–1965), who regarded his own compositions as "musical space as open rather than bounded," which would be an apt description of Zappa's music.[1]

In addition to providing a summary and overview of the origins of progressive rock in the late 1960s, *Experiencing Progressive Rock: A Listener's Companion* takes the reader further into the developments that were starting in the 1990s in Europe, Scandinavia, and the United States among a new generation of variously rock-styled musicians who were drawing on the influences of progressive rock music of their own youth or even that of their parents and who no longer provided limiting categorizations to their bands in the same way that progressive record companies did in the late 1960s through the 1980s. Instead, bands such as Dream Theater (formed in 1986), Meshuggah, Porcupine Tree, and Cynic (all of which formed in 1987, although Steven Wilson, the leader of Porcupine Tree, continues to perform as a solo artist, albeit with his own band), Opeth (formed in 1990), Between the Buried and Me (formed in 2000), and Animals As Leaders (formed in 2007) compose and perform music that at once demonstrates extreme musical virtuosity as well as a broad mix of musics, all of which embrace the styles (examples in following chapters) that once defined any individual progressive band. Equally, solo progressive performers broke ground that had previously been the domain of the "pop singer" singing three-minute songs and who most often did not compose. Singer and songwriter-performer Kate Bush is an example of a performer encouraged by her record company to combine sophisticated songwriting techniques with elaborate stage performances, achieving success in the single and album charts between the late 1970s and 1980s. She also collaborated with Peter Gabriel and David Gilmour.

That said, the term "progressive," a media term used by record companies when applied to a style of music in the late 1960s and 1970s, implied that a band or solo performer combined core rock origins with a style that did not come from the roots music of the 1950s and had not been a part of the blues revival that had recently occurred on both sides of the Atlantic. The list of examples throughout this work is, again, not comprehensive but serves to illustrate how bands in this genre were pigeonholed by fans and record companies alike. The limitation of being described as "classical rock" was, and often still is, applied to the Nice, Procol Harum (which released a new album at the time of writing in 2017), Emerson, Lake and Palmer, Gryphon, early Electric Light Orchestra, some King Crimson, some Van der Graaf Generator, Barclay James Harvest, and the Enid. The Enid is particularly interesting because, like Genesis at Charterhouse School, the members met at school; in the Enid's case, it was Finchden Manor in Kent. This school had a mixture of musicians who left and enjoyed careers in various musical styles, including the 1980s rock singer Tom Robinson. Enid bassist Terry Pack told me that the band was "controlled" by Robert John Godfrey, an authoritarian musician who had attended the Royal College of Music (musical education being common to many of the musicians interviewed for this book); his manner caused many personnel changes during the band's lengthy career and "most normal people would only put up with so much abuse before packing their bags."[2] The band still performs and has recorded several albums during its existence, a commonality that arises throughout this book.

As stated earlier, "progressive rock" was originally a media and recording company marketing term used to describe the various combinations of rock music of the time with music from other stylistic areas. The term is often a matter of contention nowadays, an issue discussed in later chapters. Though some published works focus mainly on the combination of classical music with rock, this view limits what progressive rock became, and record companies and other media "manufactured" several other descriptions of the fusions that emerged. Examples include "jazz-rock," the progressive term used to describe bands such as Soft Machine, which at various times included Allan Holdsworth and John Etheridge, two British guitarists who, along with John McLaughlin of the Mahavishnu Orchestra, helped shape jazz-rock on both sides of the Atlantic throughout the 1970s and 1980s. McLaughlin and Holdsworth also played in Tony Williams's Lifetime. Tempest was a band that featured Patto guitarist Ollie Halsall, Holdsworth, and Jon Hiseman of Colosseum on drums. These bands, along with Nucleus, Isotope, If, Egg, Caravan, Hatfield and the North, and the National Health, are only a few of many other jazz-rock bands under the U.K. progressive rock marketing umbrella, and they do not include the bands led in the United States by ex–Miles Davis sidemen such as Chick Corea, Tony Williams, and Josef Zawinul (McLaughlin, a British musician who had performed with Davis and led the Mahavishnu Orchestra, which was U.S. based). "Afro rock" was used as a marketing description for Osibisa, and "folk-rock" was used as a marketing tool for Fairport Convention, Steeleye Span, Gryphon, the Strawbs, and the Albion Band. "Eastern rock" (surprisingly not "Asian rock") was the description for Quintessence, although many other bands also drew on Indian and other Asian influences in the wake of the use of "world" music influences by bands such as the Beatles, the Rolling Stones, and Led Zeppelin. Again, these pigeonhole descriptions were mostly created by the media and record companies of the period under the broader umbrella term "progressive rock." An issue that becomes apparent here is that many progressive rock bands, no matter the styles from which they were originally influenced, were often formed from combinations of musicians from already established bands, thus providing fertile ground for experimentation, virtuosity, and conceptuality, issues that are discussed throughout this work.

Considering that several of the virtuoso guitarists of progressive rock had their origins in the blues revivals mentioned earlier, it is not surprising that "blues rock" was also considered a progressive rock style, the Groundhogs and Steamhammer being two popular bands that blended blues with thematic songwriting. Led Zeppelin and Cream had also started their respective careers drawing influences from the blues. However, when one listens to bands such as Deep Purple (with a classically trained keyboard player, Jon Lord, and a blues-based guitarist, Ritchie Blackmore), Led Zeppelin (with Robert Plant and Jimmy Page's combined interests in folk-music of the British Isles and the influences they amassed on their trips to North Africa, combined with blues influences), the addition of the "blues" description would seem to be apparent to many progressive bands from Cream onward. I add Cream because of their musical experimentation on "I Feel Free" (1966), *Disraeli Gears* (1967), and *Wheels of Fire* (1968), albums with a combination of blues ("Crossroads" and "Sitting on Top of the World") but also with the complexity of "As You Said," "Those Were the Days," and "Deserted Cities of the Heart." Equally, the complexity of Led Zeppelin's material, especially their anthem "Stairway to Heaven," pushed the boundaries of heavier progressive, and dynamically arranged, rock. Thus, despite the efforts of record companies and the popular publications of the period to categorize bands, progressive rock became a multi-styled genre that was at once eclectic, a significant progressive rock description, with many bands borrowing from several styles yet also quite often closely allied to a single influence outside rock music of the period.

From a mainland European perspective, the Dutch band Focus featured the organ and flute of the classically trained keyboard player and composer, Thijs van Leer (who also yodeled on some of the band's recordings), whose playing was juxtaposed with the jazz-rock influenced guitar of Jan Akkerman. The Italian band PFM (Premiata Forneria Marconi) combined classical music with Italian traditional music and often performed covers of King Crimson tunes.

SETTING THE SCENE

The history of the origins of progressive rock in the late 1960s and 1970s has been well documented (for example, Paul Stump, Edward Macan, Bill Wilson, and Martin Halliwell and Paul Hegarty).[3] Equally, the Beatles' move away from the three-minute single format to album conceptuality involving longer compositions has been comprehensively documented by Ian MacDonald.[4] It therefore is not my intention to expand the content of these works. Instead, in chapter 1—and to an extent in chapter 2—I outline the growth of student-based enthusiasm for progressive rock in its early stages from a personal perspective, and I add anecdotes from some of the established performers of the period, some of whom are still performing in the same bands and others who have formed new bands. Several scholars correctly have noted that some progressive rock bands emerged from the psychedelia of the late 1960s, Pink Floyd being a prominent example (although this description was no longer valid following the release of *Dark Side of the Moon* [1973] and later albums). Psychedelic presentation was, however, apparent in the early stages of progressive rock, especially in lighting. My choice of progressive rock bands in this book instead focuses on bands that formed purposely to combine rock music with other styles of music that had been studied formally or that were simply a musical choice based on the tastes of a band's members. I offer my apologies for not being able to provide more information on all of the bands I include in the discussion that follows.

SOME INFORMATION ABOUT THE AUTHOR AND WHAT FOLLOWS IN LATER CHAPTERS

Prior to discussing what progressive music actually was—or, indeed, what it is—I must indulge in a short account of my personal introduction to music prior to becoming a professional musician in order to put this guide to the progressive rock genre into context and to provide information on my access to my interviewees.

The United Kingdom Education Act of 1944 raised the age at which students leave school to age fifteen and established a secondary education system based on students being sent to one of three types of schools following the "eleven-plus" exam taken at the age of eleven. This exam effectively decided the life status of those who took it. Those who passed went to grammar schools, which were regarded as being for the academically inclined and who were destined for tertiary education, which was mostly free. It therefore reinforced the social divide in line with the class system that had always existed in the United Kingdom, particularly under conservative governments. Those who failed the eleven-plus went either to technical schools (for those destined for practical apprenticeships) or secondary modern schools, which, due to the larger number of "failed" students, attracted most funding.

I grew up in fear of the eleven-plus and, being an only child, I felt parental pressure to pass. Fate intervened, however, and in the mid-1960s, the exam was abolished in favor of an assessment of one's last two years of schoolwork. I was thus admitted to a staid grammar school within approximately twenty-five miles of London with Greco-Roman architecture, wherein one studied the classics with several elderly staff, some of whom had fought in World War II and maintained 1930s and 1940s social and cultural values. My parents had predetermined my career to be that of a medical practitioner, but at the end of the second year I was placed into the liberal arts stream that focused on arts, languages, and, most importantly, music. Although parental pressure toward the sciences never really stopped (even after I became a professional musician at the age of nineteen), my educational progress in French, German, and music became apparent. I took Saturday morning trumpet lessons from a member of the London Symphony Orchestra, and with the ongoing encouragement of the school's own music teacher, I received what I still regard as an excellent beginning to my eventual musical career. Having been asked to join the school orchestra, my interest in what I will refer to from now on as "classical music"(despite its status as a musical period rather than a description of a genre) grew and I became familiar, through theory lessons and performances, with what are often referred to by classical music lovers as "the great works," which was reinforced by the playing of a classical recording or a live student performance during each morning's assembly.

As well as studying classical music, I listened to pop music on Radio Luxembourg, the offshore "radio pirates" such as Radio Caroline and Radio London, and what little pop music the BBC Light Programme broadcast in the mid-1960s prior to its liberalization as "Radio 1." I thus assumed that all pop songs were quite simple in construction and that they were all about three minutes in duration. During one school music lesson, however, the music teacher asked us to select and focus on one group of instruments on a recording. The piece was composed by J. S. Bach and I chose to listen to the bass line, which seemed to me the most melodic part. I tried to explain, as all the students had to, why I had chosen it, and the best I could manage was its melodic movement and almost visceral qualities. Later that week, I was reading a U.K. music newspaper, *Melody Maker* (another part of my future experiences, since this publication listed bands that needed musicians), about one of my favourite bands, Cream, whose music seemed far more complex than most other bands at the time, perhaps with the exception of the Beatles. The interview I read was with bass guitarist Jack Bruce (a friend in later life) who said that his own musical education on double bass had been highly influenced by Bach, even when he had discovered jazz and blues and had become one of the most sought-after bassists in London. And that was it. I had to play bass, but not just *play*, I had to be able to *create* music, something I could not do on the trumpet. I found in the interviews that follow that I was not alone.

My "rock epiphany" was similar to that of some of my informants in this book, and it occurred long before I became a professional musician. As a tokenistic nod to the growth of the popularity of pop and rock music, my school permitted a weekly record club to be held during lunchtime. Students were encouraged to bring an LP to the club and present a discussion on it while playing selected tracks. The club was for students in the fifth and sixth forms, although I was smuggled in by older friends. These occasions introduced me to the British blues revival driven by Alexis Korner and, in particular, John Mayall's Bluesbreakers, which at the time had guitarist Eric Clapton in their ranks. The musical turning point for me was Clapton's overdriven Marshall combo that, as legend has it, was turned up to maximum volume to achieve the sound he wanted. Hearing that album broadened my musical tastes beyond classical and the lighter pop music that was broadcast on public radio of the time and made me aware of virtuosity in a rock music context. In other words, virtuosity was not solely in the domain of the classical music with which I was familiar. Another epiphany occurred one Sunday afternoon when I visited a cousin's house. He had started a job at a local bank and had received his first paycheck, with which he purchased the Beatles' *Sgt. Pepper's Lonely Hearts Club Band* (1967) and *Are You Experienced* (1967) by the Jimi Hendrix Experience. We listened to both albums several times in one sitting, and I remember walking home with a very different view of my career plans and a determination to study what made this music different from what I was already studying.

I had already persuaded my parents to buy me an electric bass guitar, but playing this instrument every evening had transcended "fun"; I now took to the instrument with a seriousness that I had never dedicated to my trumpet. I had recorded my cousin's new albums (unaware of the copyright issues), some Who recordings ("My Generation" [1965] and the album *A Quick One* [1966]), as well as a bass-centric single, "Keep on Running," by the Spencer Davis Group. These tracks became the first lines I ever played on bass.

I also started attending the weekly concerts that were presented at my local concert hall, as well as attending Deep Purple's *Concerto for Group and Orchestra* (1969) at the Royal Albert Hall in London. Significantly, it was at my local venue that I discovered how to get backstage, and I made a point of talking to as many of the musicians who performed there as possible. Some of them became musical colleagues in my later professional life (for example, Viv Stanshall of the Bonzo Dog Band, Keith Moon, and Tim Renwick, then with Junior's Eyes but more recently with Pink Floyd and several others).

Although my schoolwork rarely suffered (other than the ringing in my ears the day after each concert, particularly one by the Who), I was determined to be a musician, and progressive rock held the musical challenges for me that drove my hours of practicing. Another factor that supported this new student-based genre was BBC Radio 1's weekly broadcast of *Top Gear* on Sunday afternoons (which I also recorded to broaden my growing collection of progressive rock music repertoire that was not always available on vinyl).[5] This program was presented by John Peel (1939–2004), a broadcaster who was enthusiastic about the experimental nature of progressive rock in all its styles and who was largely responsible for its growing popularity at the time. Many unknown bands whose demo tapes he broadcast went on to successful careers.

By this time, I had also developed an eclectic view of what progressive rock was becoming. I was listening to the folk-rock of Fairport

Convention, whose guitarist Richard Thompson's virtuosity arguably rivaled that of Jimi Hendrix and Jimmy Page (Simon Nicol of Fairport Convention later told me that Thompson often jammed with both of them at London's elite Speakeasy Club).[6] Through Fairport, I discovered the guitar expertise of Martin Carthy, who would eventually join Fairport spinoff, Steeleye Span. I also listened to the guitar experimentation of post-Yardbirds Jeff Beck (despite what I regarded as a fall from grace with "Hi Ho Silver Lining"). It was on Peel's radio show, however, that I first heard the full orchestral version of the Moody Blues' "Nights in White Satin" (1967), which was recorded with the London Festival Orchestra and, more significantly, was a rough mix (i.e., not the final released version) of King Crimson's "In the Court of the Crimson King." The band had, at the time, only done a handful of live performances, including one at Friars Club in Aylesbury, near London, before they signed with EG Records, which licensed the band to the newly founded Island Records, a label that became synonymous with progressive rock. Friars Club was one of the most iconic progressive music venues in the late 1960s and 1970s and, being near London, attracted record company personnel. Peel personally played recorded music in the role of what was once referred to as a "disc jockey," and as stated earlier, many of the live bands that performed there were then featured on his radio show and were often given recording contracts.

The following chapter therefore discusses six progressive rock bands of the late 1960s and early 1970s that were extremely influential to the growth in popularity of the progressive rock genre and that continue to tour in the 2000s.

Although my own experience of progressive rock was initially as part of Allan F. Moore's "student-based" following (more descriptions of that later), I spent most of my life since my late teenage years as a professional bassist. I worked in recording studios and did several world tours over three decades, being fortunate to perform at various times with David Gilmour and other members of Pink Floyd, Pete Townshend, Jon Lord and Ian Paice, Jerry Donahue (Fairport Convention), Eric Burdon (the Animals), Ian Carr's Nucleus, James Burton (Elvis Presley), Albert Lee (Emmylou Harris; Eric Clapton), Bob Weston (Fleetwood Mac), Snowy White (Thin Lizzy), Clem Clempson (Colosseum), Jakko Jakszyk (King Crimson), and Robin Lumley (Brand X). I also played on many television program soundtracks, such as *Mr. Bean*,

Blackadder, and *Red Dwarf*. Thus, my professional experience—which started as a "hired gun" for visiting American soul performers in the 1970s and included work for Isaac Hayes, Sam and Dave, and the Stylistics—was always broad in terms of the styles I was asked to play. Progressive rock and its many spinoffs were, however, always central to my continual need to move with the developments of bass playing—and these came principally from progressive rock and one of its later incarnations, jazz-rock (also known as "fusion," which stemmed from the music of Miles Davis in the late 1960s). I therefore start this book from a slightly autoethnographic perspective, describing my own experiences and the inspiration that I obtained from a nearly continual diet of progressive rock during my formative years. That said, I still listen to this music that inspired me in my youth and its evolution that has been driven by some of the more recent bands already mentioned. Due to my professional career, I have been able to draw on anecdotes from my former colleagues, most of whom are now close friends, as well as their recollections and views on how progressive rock has developed to the present day.

Early chapters in this book expand on growth and decline in progressive rock, particularly during the 1970s and its revival during the 1980s, because, contrary to some published opinion, the genre did survive the punk, new wave, romantic, and electronic styles that followed in later years, some of which Allan F. Moore has described as "the working-class dancing market."[7] These chapters include analytical discussions about songs recorded in various areas of progressive rock and the advances in recording and performance technologies that enabled "progression." Chapter 6 discusses "new" progressive rock bands (as well as some that are borderline progressive) that have emerged since the early 1990s that embrace metal-oriented styles, and chapter 7 looks at the issue of spectacle, a concept mostly in the domain of the most established progressive bands. Chapter 8 considers what happens when established bands reunite after periods of hiatus. Anecdotes included in chapters 9 and 10 come from contemporary performers who either embraced progressive rock, having been influenced by the original progressive bands, or have played progressive rock since the 1970s and have taken the genre in new directions while maintaining the conceptuality, musical curiosity, and virtuosity—central trademarks of the style.

Given the change in how music has been distributed since the 1990s, musical descriptions do not seem to be such an important factor for some musicians, especially because bands of any style formulate their own music, a point of further discussion in later chapters.

The terms used to describe contemporary rock music are vaguer than the genres of the 1970s, and the term "heavy metal," as described by both Deena Weinstein and by Robert Walser, is now, to an extent, outmoded.[8] Although both authors describe the fragmentation of metal styles from the heavy metal of, for example, Black Sabbath, Iron Maiden, and Metallica, among others, the "metal" guitar-driven styles have become ever more eclectic—"speed," "thrash," "death," "nu," and "tech" all being examples of this new diversity—and the process is ongoing. In terms of contemporary progressive rock, the trend toward combining influences and constant invention and reinvention also continues into the present, some of it influenced by the change in metal styles from the perspective of guitar playing (although this change is broad and is discussed in a later chapter), as well as by new technologies and the increased availability of popular music education in fields of performance, composition, the music industry, and the use of music software. There are many relatively new progressive rock bands not included here that are discussed in later chapters. Some of these bands cite earlier bands as primary influences, others regard their musical repertoire as a current musical statement that has a sense of ownership within the particular band that inevitably develops as a band continues to perform together. The most significant point here, however, is that progressive rock (although the term "rock" can be problematic, because it encompasses so many genres nowadays) still progresses.

MY INFORMANTS AND THEIR MUSICAL BACKGROUNDS

The musical backgrounds and experiences of some of my former colleagues in the music industry who have kindly assisted me in the investigation carried out for this book are worthy of attention. Much of the research I have carried out stems from conversations, sometimes over several years, as well as from recent interviews, and the information I have gleaned therefore comes from the practitioners of the genre either from informal sharing of memories or from recent formal interviews.

All of the information here comes from musicians who have worked at the highest levels of progressive rock, some of whom are still doing so.

During the 1990s, I performed with guitarist Clem Clempson of Colosseum, who had also played with Jack Bruce during the 1980s and in the 1990s (for example, *Cities of the Heart* [1994]). He told me that his introduction to the study of music as a child was through piano lessons. He described how the influence of what might be described as classical music gave way to the visceral nature of 1950s and 1960s popular music that was guitar based:

> [My earliest influences were] Beethoven, Tchaikovsky, etcetera, and everything I heard on the radio in the 1950s, from the "Third Man" theme to the Everly Brothers and Buddy Holly, but especially "Rock around the Clock"—an aunt took me to see the movie when I was around seven or eight, and that's what sparked my fascination with the electric guitar. [9]

Clempson had been asked to join Colosseum after his own band, Bakerloo, had supported Colosseum several times. Though Colosseum has clear jazz and jazz fusion influences, Clempson maintained his own blues influences, combining them with his admiration for John McLaughlin of the Mahavishnu Orchestra and Robert Fripp of King Crimson. Diversity in Clempson's playing is apparent in the live version of "Valentyne Suite Part Three: The Grass Is Always Greener" (his favorite Colosseum song), which is discussed later in this chapter.

I had a similar discussion with another progressive rock guitarist with whom I also performed in the 1990s. John Knightsbridge had played in the Yardbirds, but his progressive reputation came to the fore with Rick Wakeman, Third World War, Renaissance, Illusion, and the Strawbs. Whereas Clempson described a mixture of formal classical music education combined with what he heard on the radio and at the cinema, Knightsbridge was completely self-taught. Like many guitarists (and those who turned to bass), he initially studied tutor books, such as *Play in a Day* (originally published in 1957) by Bert Weedon. Weedon was a 1950s and early 1960s session guitarist who appeared on children's television programs in the early 1960s, giving short lessons that were often beyond the abilities of most children.

For Knightsbridge, Weedon was out of touch with the current styles, despite his prolific list of recording sessions, but his book did provide chord grid diagrams showing where to put one's fingers to play a chord. Knightsbridge eschewed published tutoring, preferring an autodidactic approach of listening to recordings and broadcasts and learning what he described as "lead lines" without the chords that supported them. Knightsbridge's earliest experiences were gained from learning (by ear) instrumental tunes by the Shadows and the "twangy" songs of Duane Eddy.[10] He soon found himself in local bands, particularly playing country and western music. His rock "awakening," however, was seeing blues singer and guitarist John Lee Hooker. This experience led to an interest in jazz, and Knightsbridge cites the Modern Jazz Quartet, Jimmy Smith, and Oscar Peterson in the development of his musical technique. Like most young guitarists of the period, he learned by listening rather than by formal instruction, but this led to his first professional engagement as a lead and rhythm guitarist in a band performing in Germany, a country that seemed to be a rite of passage for many future progressive rock musicians.

Other informants were also varied in terms of their introduction to music and indeed to progressive rock. I spoke with Nick Beggs, a bassist who is also an in-demand Chapman stick player (a ten-stringed instrument that works as both a guitar and bass and that can perform a similar role to a keyboard; the strings are tapped by the performer using fingers on both hands). Beggs's early career was in the 1980s as bassist for a successful pop band, Kajagoogoo, but he started to study music theory later in life because, as he says,

> I was self-taught up to the age of twenty-five. After that I realized I needed to learn more theory if I was going to be able to make a living as a musician and not just be an "artist." It was a slow crossover. But it's notable that I have played with many genres of music over my thirty-two year career—funk, soul, pop, rock, gospel, Celtic folk, a little jazz, blues, world music, aspects of classical music, and cabaret. Prog was an inevitability at some point, I guess.[11]

Beggs's increasing musical knowledge—and, indeed, his instrumental virtuosity—brought him to the attention of former Led Zeppelin bassist John Paul Jones through a recommendation from King Crimson's Robert Fripp.

> John Paul Jones [said] he had been a fan of Kajagoogoo in the 1980s, so he was aware of my playing. When it came time for him to put his solo band together, he thought of me, and as he had just signed to Disciple Records, Robert Fripp also suggested me. It was Robert who actually called me up and offered me the chair. That project taught me more than I ever could have imagined. It was a priceless experience and John became a dear friend.[12]

It seems, therefore, that formal music education could be gained once a musician already had become established, the variation of introductions to professional musicianship becoming even more varied. Beggs is currently the bassist for Steven Wilson and performs and records on Wilson's tours. Beggs also performs with former Genesis guitarist Steve Hackett and with his own band, the Mute Gods. Due to his prolific activities and prestigious reputation, he was awarded the Classic Rock Society Bass Player of the Year Award for three years running (2015, 2016, and 2017).

Another variation of musical background in progressive rock is Gary O'Toole, a drummer whose musical background stemmed not from formal musical education, but from his musical family. He described his early experiences.

> I was brought up playing gigs, [and] from the age of four, I was always singing. I thought singing was too easy and one had to work to be a musician. So I tried piano then guitar, and at age ten I began playing bass with my parent's trio. I was rubbish but I got lots of attention as I was young. My parents both loved jazz, and I was open to early Dave Brubeck, Oscar Peterson, Art Tatum, Val Doonican, and Russ Conway. It's all there! We played workingmen's clubs and pubs. When I reached twelve, Dad said he was actually the bass player and the trio needed a drummer. I continued to hold a bass on gigs till I was fourteen, when I first really discovered playing drums.[13]

As with Beggs, O'Toole's early career was established by performing with pop bands, although a relative had already introduced him to progressive rock and jazz: "He got me listening to ELP [Emerson, Lake and Palmer], Yes, Genesis, King Crimson, as well as all the great jazz drummers, Buddy Rich, Louie Belson, Tony Williams, Art Blakey, Max Roach. . . . There were so many."[14]

Like Beggs, O'Toole came to the realization that, in order to enter a higher level of musicianship (and thus employment) opportunities, more work had to be done in terms of his technique. This work paid off and he gradually entered the professional world.

> I began playing gigs away from my family in 1978, I guess. Rock mainly, and other covers gigs. Then one thing led to another and it began with a couple of gigs with Sweet Sensation [a successful British pop band]. After that I realized I needed to work harder and got into more bands learning about "keeping the groove." I would play with big bands now and then, as I loved the challenge of reading. From there I had a chance to dep [stand in for] in the West End show *Cats*. I kept that "dep" seat from 1983 until the show closed around 2003. I also got the gig with pop band China Crisis [another successful British pop band], who did some serious tours of their own and supported the Police and Simple Minds. That was real experience. I learned the difference between being a sideman and being part of the band. I later did a number of gigs with Big Chief with Tony Reeves and Dick Heckstall-Smith [both formerly of Colosseum before the band reunited]. A couple of times, as Dick's health declined, John Etheridge [of Soft Machine] would play guitar, and we would take it out there. At this point, I was not good enough to be in the swim with the big boys, but I knew it and was practicing.[15]

O'Toole is now the drummer and vocalist in former Genesis guitarist Steve Hackett's band and sings Peter Gabriel's vocal parts while playing drums. Although some musicians playing progressive rock—particularly that rooted in classical music—required an introduction to certain styles by way of formal education, others found support and guidance from musical experience within a family setting. Still other musicians adopted a more autodidactic approach based on early listening experiences and a personal desire for musical improvement.

Yet another informant had no music education at all, and his entire musical career has been based on his love of progressive rock and a wariness of entering a business career. Rick Fenn has played guitar and sung in 10cc since 1977, a band that I refer to as "progressive pop." (I explain the terms used to describe progressive rock in greater depth in a later chapter.) He described his early years as follows:

I never had any musical education to speak of. Nor did I get much encouragement from home, but Hendrix and Cream consolidated my obsession with guitar in my early teens.

I had a school band and a college band called Bagshot Louie and Pariah respectively, but when I left Cambridge Technical College in '74, clutching my HND [Higher National Diploma] in business studies and the dawning realization that I might actually have to get a job in business, I joined the first serious band that would have me.

And so, for the two to three years before I was invited into 10cc, I was in the proggiest prog rock band you could imagine called Gentlemen. We lived together, shared our dole cheques [checks], and discouraged girlfriends, as they were a distraction from our intensely myopic ambitions. Yes and Genesis were the two main gods that we worshipped. Within the genre, we were pretty good, I suppose, and if the tide had not turned on prog rock, it's possible we would have gotten a break, but come the punk Armageddon in '76, we didn't stand a chance.[16]

Despite radio broadcasts and television performances, the band foundered, but not before the band employed Paul Burgess, the 10cc drummer, who later joined Camel and Jethro Tull as a session musician. Fenn and Burgess became friends and, when Kevin Godley and Lol Crème left the band in 1976, Burgess suggested Fenn as a replacement guitarist for Crème (the band had often used two drummers for recording and touring and Burgess was by now a permanent member). Fenn has been a member ever since, performing on recordings and tours for the band. Again, the differences in musical backgrounds among progressive rock musicians becomes ever more varied. In 1985, Fenn composed and performed with David Gilmour and Nick Mason on the album *Profiles*.

Another informant is drummer and percussionist Paul Burgess of 10cc, who has a similar background, although he had a formal introduction to music. His early musical experiences were piano lessons in the early 1960s, but he started playing drums in 1965 and joined friends in a group playing songs by the Beatles and the Monkees before becoming part of the British blues revival, despite his youth. Burgess became a professional musician in 1971 and was mentored by an older professional drummer in his home city of Manchester, a significant area in which to live, given his musical future in 10cc. As well as being given work by his mentor, Burgess was introduced to a wide range of rock music of the time.

> I was introduced to the music of a lot of American bands like Steppenwolf, Three Dog Night, Frank Zappa, Captain Beefheart, the Tubes, and the Doors, but hearing King Curtis (with Bernard Purdie on drums) was a turning point for me, and soul, funk, and jazz rock then became the main influence on my playing style ever since. My first encounter with prog came in 1972, when I was recruited by Ankh [a Manchester band that became Sad Café, which had several hit albums and singles and is still touring] to record an album, some of it at Strawberry Studios. There, I met Eric Stewart and Graham Gouldman, and the following year they asked me to join their new band, 10cc, as a touring member.[17]

During a personal break from 10cc in 1982, Burgess joined Jethro Tull, during which time 10cc made a new album with session drummers Steve Gadd and Simon Phillips. After Burgess's tours with Jethro Tull, he returned to 10cc, but by this time the band's music had changed and he was not fond of the new direction the band had taken. At this point, he was invited to join Camel and performed with the band until the late 1990s, when he was invited to return to 10cc by one of the founding members, bassist Graham Gouldman. He has been with the band since that time. Like Fenn, Burgess has provided insights for this work into progressive rock band longevity and how progressive styles have remained popular to the present.

One of the leading bassists in contemporary progressive rock is Tony Levin. Levin is a performer who has been at the forefront of the style since he became Peter Gabriel's bassist in the late 1970s, when Gabriel's solo career established itself. When Gabriel left Genesis following the *Lamb Lies Down on Broadway* tour in 1975, he released his first solo recording, *Car*, in 1977. This was Levin's first recording for Gabriel, despite already being a session veteran for many other performers. He described his formative years to me.

> [I was a] classical player through college (Eastman School of Music in Rochester) then played jazz and rock, moved to New York City, where I "fell into" doing recording sessions, frankly as a way to pay the bills while trying to get in a jazz or rock group.

> I heard about the Chapman stick around 1976 and thought it could give me a different sound and texture on the bass, so I was one of the early musicians to get one. Starting with Peter Gabriel's touring shortly after that, I slowly got used to playing it as a bass and only added the top side (guitar strings) after that.
>
> Some other well-known artists I've recorded with are Peter Gabriel, John Lennon, David Bowie, Pink Floyd, Paul Simon, James Taylor, Carly Simon . . . [and] quite a few more.[18]

He went on to describe the differences between his later work with King Crimson and the way in which Peter Gabriel composed his songs.

> It's quite a different experience. In Crimson, we would have written the material before going in to record. Then in the studio it was always a pretty quick process of getting good takes on the pieces. Peter, having written his music, works painstakingly on the rhythm section parts—sometimes for a month or so for the album but often reconvening a second or third time to approach things in a different way.[19]

Levin's work with King Crimson, a band with which he has worked since 1981, is discussed in detail in chapter 5, and he has now become one of the most respected bassists in the progressive genre, having also worked with members of Yes (Anderson, Bruford, Wakeman, and Howe), Dream Theater, and the Liquid Tension Experiment and has performed in an improvised fusion band with Terry Bozzio (one of Frank Zappa's drummers) and guitarist Allan Holdsworth. He is also a double bassist and played tuba on Gabriel's first solo album, as well as bass guitar.

Another member of the most recent King Crimson lineup who has helped with my research for this book is guitarist and vocalist Jakko Jakszyk, whom I first met at a charity concert in London in 1989 when we were jamming live with Robin Lumley, the keyboard player and producer of Phil Collins's band, Brand X. Jakszyk and I have been in touch intermittently since then but have been in contact more regularly with the aid of social media. Like many of my informants, his musical beginnings came from his experimentation on his father's guitar, an instrument with which he became "obsessed" by the age of eleven. At this point, he was introduced to progressive rock on an Island Records sampler (*Nice Enough to Eat* [1969], an album containing tracks from progressive bands signed to the label). The track that he says moved him most was "21st Century Schizoid Man" by King Crimson. He attended a concert by the band near London in 1971 that "blew him away." He admits that trying to play like Robert Fripp was "way above" his ability at the time, and his classical flute studies suffered because of time spent trying to play "the twisted and insane" on guitar.[20]

It is significant, however, that, like several other informants for this book, Jakszyk had undertaken formal classical music studies before pursuing progressive rock performance. Like many musicians in the 1970s, he found himself in a band entering competitions, notably the annual event sponsored by the *Melody Maker*. Again, like many bands of the period, the mercurial lineup of Jakszyk's band prevented success, and he describes himself at the time as being a "dictatorial teenager."[21] Once a consistent lineup established itself, Jakszyk's band won a heat of the competition playing his "strange instrumental compositions" and the band found itself performing at the competition's final at the Roundhouse, a well-established London rock venue. This performance gained the band management and tours supporting established progressive bands, such as Camel and Stackridge (a band discussed in a later chapter). Jakszyk went on to join a band called 64 Spoons, which consisted of classically trained musicians who used odd time signatures, a familiar trend in progressive rock, and syncopated rhythms. He regards being the guitarist and vocalist in this band as his "real education," and the band lasted for four years. His next band was with members of Hatfield and the North, a spinoff from Caravan, Matching Mole, and Gong.

Later in his career, he became a commercial songwriter, and his publisher put him in touch with Peter Sinfield, King Crimson's first lyricist, who had had recent success writing for Diana Ross and Celine Dion. Although their collaboration did not achieve success, it was inevitable that Jakszyk and Sinfield would discuss the early years of King Crimson. This was a period of synchronicity for Jakszyk, as Sinfield introduced him to Robert Fripp and other members of the band (significantly, Sinfield introduced Jakszyk as a guitarist who "could re-create Robert's parts"). Jakszyk was eventually invited to record with Fripp, and the result was an album called *A Scarcity of Miracles* (2011), featuring bassist Levin, Gavin Harrison on drums, and Mel Collins on saxophone (a veteran of earlier King Crimson lineups). This ensemble then became the current King Crimson. [22]

Steven Wilson, a highly respected composer, producer, performer, and multi-instrumentalist, differs from most of the musicians mentioned earlier in terms of musical training. His prolific output with his band, Porcupine Tree, and, more recently, works released under his own name has been the product of thirty years of work. Yet in an interview, he said:

> I played piano and I played guitar, and my parents forced me to go to lessons [he said he preferred football]. And I learned nothing and I hated it. In fact, it had the opposite effect. I stopped playing piano and I stopped playing guitar because I hated it so much. . . . I can't read music, and I don't have any academic training. I don't know the names of the chords I play. Sometimes it's like teaching the band some of the music and I'm like, "Well, this is this chord." And Adam Holzman [Wilson's keyboard player] will probably say, "Ah, you're playing A, diminished four." And I'm like, "Well, whatever." But I know the shape and I know how it sounds, but I don't know the name of it. But you don't need to. [23]

Wilson's current work is discussed in depth in a later chapter, but his views on progressive rock are of great significance. Of equal significance are his views on the combination of soundscape and artwork in his outputs, as well as his ideas about surround sound mixing and the sound quality produced by vinyl.

Finally, Robin Lumley, a keyboard player who has performed with Phil Collins, Peter Gabriel, and produced and performed with Brand X, told me about his musical beginnings and his personal means of becoming a keyboard player of high regard. He explained how he was self-taught from books and listening to records. He played at home with a Hohner Pianet N (a basic electric piano of the 1960s and 1970s), along with his favorite keyboard players by listening to recordings. Significantly, he used "plenty of scale books."[24]

Robin's "first big gig" was as pianist in the stage shows for Ziggy Stardust and the Spiders from Mars, and he stated that he "certainly learn[ed] a lot from David and Mick Ronson, including a lot of new (to me) chords." He then entered a period of composition, recording with partner Jack Lancaster and worked with a studio band that included future members of Brand X, John Goodsall on guitar and Percy Jones on bass. Other members included guitarist Gary Moore and drummer Bill Bruford. Lumley and Lancaster then recorded and produced a rock version of Prokofiev's *Peter and the Wolf* (1975) and *Marscape* (1976); significantly, the studio band now included Phil Collins. These recordings led to other Lancaster solo projects for various record labels, though the combination of musicians remained essentially the same but also included Rod Argent (who is discussed in a later chapter) and Clive Bunker, the drummer from Jethro Tull. The flexibility in project and band personnel combinations is a progressive rock issue that, again, is discussed later. Several of the musicians from these sessions decided to form Brand X, a jazz rock (a term used by record companies under the umbrella of progressive rock) group, which for Lumley "was a very fulfilling eight years and [we undertook] multiple albums and U.S./ European live tours [and were awarded] three Melody Maker awards."[25] These awards included Best Jazz Act Melody Maker (1978, 1979, and 1980), and Lumley was also personally awarded the 1979 Best Original Keyboardist Newcomer by *Contemporary Keyboards* magazine and the 1989 Best Music for TV Commercial/Best Produced Music TV Commercial by the Independent Advertising Awards for the Natural Sounds Music category. Lumley's career has thus been varied, although as with many of my other interviewees, he has firm views about the meaning of "progressive" when applied to rock, and in his case, any other style.

In conclusion, a definition of progressive rock music remains problematic for my interviewees—many of whom eschew the term—even though it has become a standard term for music containing various elements of virtuosity, complexity, stylistic mixes, and other factors. Nevertheless, the next chapter initially attempts to focus on the genre in the earliest stages of its existence. It discusses a number of progressive bands who became established in the 1970s and whose careers have spanned more than four decades.

I

"FROM THE BEGINNING"
The Struggle for Definition

This chapter illustrates how progressive rock emerged as a distinct entity in the wake of albums by bands whose record companies were not concerned with producing three-minute hit songs. Record companies, both major and independent, of the late 1960s and 1970s that facilitated this change promoted complex "rock" music to a listening audience rather than a dancing audience. It is also worth noting Frank Zappa's firm views about progressive rock, given his own struggles with record companies in the early days of the Mothers of Invention, which was not a "singles" band and whose experimental music is extremely hard to define. In a television interview in 1984, Zappa was asked to define his own music as well as that of several other genres, one of which was progressive rock. He maintained that progressive rock was anything that did not sound like "'regular rock,' a style that just sounds like itself, all songs that sound the same, like everything on MTV, everything on the radio, that's rock. Progressive rock is stuff that doesn't sound like that."[1] Zappa made this statement almost as an affront to what he saw as the commercialization of rock music brought about by the media (particularly MTV), and his tone in the interview carries a great deal of sarcasm on this subject. When asked to define the styles of Procol Harum, Traffic, Pink Floyd, Genesis, Emerson, Lake and Palmer, Jethro Tull, King Crimson, Yes, and Devo, he said that Procol Harum, Traffic, and Devo are not progressive rock and the rest are "sometimes" progressive (the interviewer's inclusion of Devo is, admittedly, highly questionable). He did not describe his own music as progressive in the same interview, stating that sometimes "it's not even rock and roll at all; it just happens to be consumed by a rock and roll audience."

An issue that arose in progressive rock's early stages, however, was that progressive rock bands tried to elevate rock music into the realm of high art. Jay Keister and Jeremy L. Smith describe a sleeve statement on a Gentle Giant album, *Acquiring the Taste* (1971), that caused controversy among rock music critics and certain factions of the rock audience at the time: "it is our goal to expand the frontiers of contemporary popular music at the risk of being unpopular. . . . From the outset we have abandoned all preconceived thoughts on blatant commercialism. Instead we hope to give you something far more substantial and fulfilling. All you have to do is sit back and acquire the taste."[2]

Keister and Smith add that, "Commentators have had a field day with this statement. Here from the mouths of musicians themselves was an expression of all the elitism and pretension that betrayed rock's supposed adolescent populism."[3]

Given the student-based progressive audience in which there was a certain amount of musical and cultural elitism, the same might be said about many of the progressive band members. For example, Genesis formed at Charterhouse School, Curved Air had members who attended the Royal Academy of Music and the Royal College of Music, and Rick Wakeman and the folk-rock band Gryphon also attended the Royal College of Music. There is no doubt that the progressive rock audience had pretensions of musical elitism, because much of the progressive rock audience attended tertiary institutions. Simon Nicol of Fairport Convention and Ed Bicknell, manager of Dire Straits and former entertainment secretary at the University of Hull in the late 1960s and early 1970s, have both described the number of progressive bands that played at universities and colleges in the United Kingdom in the early years of the genre and agreed that it was these institutions that were the "bread and butter" gigs for progressive rock bands.[4] As part of what might be perceived as "elitism" and "pretension," progressive rock albums also provided much more information in sleeve notes than their pop, or even classical, counterparts. It is significant that although many pop performers used the session musicians of the day, progressive rock bands performed on recordings and in live performance themselves, only using session musicians to augment established lineups. Hence, Ian MacDonald's *Revolution in the Head* (1994) makes for fascinating reading because it lists all the musicians—jazz, world, and classical—used by the Beatles to create their later recordings. My own investigations among former colleagues and other established progressive rock performers suggest that most progressive musicians, whether trained or self-taught, brought influences from a broad variety of musics, such as classical, jazz, blues, avant-garde, and folk music. As stated, guitarists were often experienced in playing electric blues, having performed in the rhythm and blues revival of the 1960s, and keyboard players often had classical backgrounds. A conclusion could be, therefore, that whereas popular music styles of the period were driven by record companies; the rhythm and blues records that came from the United States; and, to an extent, the fashions of the day from both sides of the Atlantic, it was inevitable that progressive rock would enjoy the freedom to be experimental and not be confined to mainstream record company demands. It built an audience that was aware of the origins of what it was listening to and that expected a level of musicianship that became increasingly virtuosic while reflecting the cultural changes of the period.

By the mid-1970s when the punk genre became popular, it was virtuosity and musical excess that meant that only very successful progressive rock bands such as Pink Floyd, Yes, and Genesis would survive the period. This issue is discussed in chapter 4.

FROM THE SINGLE TO THE LONG PLAYER

The progressive genre was also driven by advances in studio and live sound reproduction technologies. This aspect of progressive rock, as well as how the various components of the genre were defined, is discussed in chapter 3. Suffice to say at this point, the Beatles' release of *Sgt. Pepper's Lonely Hearts Club Band*, an album that has become regarded as their artistic pinnacle of achievement, remains a major influence for many rock musicians, as does *Pet Sounds* (1966) (an album conceptualized by Brian Wilson and largely performed by session musicians but released as a Beach Boys album). *Sgt. Pepper* had been recorded at Abbey Road Recording Studios at the same time as the psychedelia of Pink Floyd's *Piper at the Gates of Dawn* and during the early sessions of *SF Sorrow*, the departure album of former blues band, the Pretty Things, from their blues roots into their own version of the psychedelic counterculture (this album was completed in 1968 while the Beatles were working on *The Beatles* and Pink Floyd on *Saucerful of Secrets*). There is still a great deal of discussion on the transition from psychedelic rock to progressive rock, and there are many lurid descriptions in rock autobiographies and biographies of experimental drug taking and successful and unsuccessful artistic results in songwriting and album production, but this is beyond the scope of this study. The aforementioned albums, however, might be labeled the precursors of what would become progressive rock.

Equally, there had already been several successful single 45 rpm recordings that featured the social commentary of Ray Davies's acerbic lyrics composed for the Kinks, Jeff Beck's guitar virtuosity in the Yardbirds, and, in terms of spectacle and instrumental aggression, Pete Townshend's use of auto-destructive art in the Who, all of which bands had hit singles between 1964 and 1967. An exception is Procol Harum's first single, the Bach-influenced "A Whiter Shade of Pale," which was released in 1967. This was followed in the same year by the successful singles, "Homburg" and then "Conquistador," which was also recorded live with the Edmonton Symphony Orchestra in 1972. Procol Harum's sophistication and musicianship, especially that of the organist, Matthew Fisher, and guitarist, Robin Trower (who joined the band after the success of "A Whiter Shade of Pale"), enabled the band to rebrand itself from its reputation as a successful U.K. "pop" band that was also successful on the U.S. charts to an album-orientated band that still tours, albeit with a different lineup. Whether the band was progressive, however, is another question. If musical virtuosity and creativity are the means by which to measure whether a band is progressive, Zappa's opinion in his television interview suggests that he may not have been familiar with several of those bands' material.

My initiation into why progressive rock music in album form might be regarded as more sophisticated than pop or standard rock, however, came when I purchased the piano transcription book of the Beatles' eponymous album (often called *The White Album* [1968]). My music teacher pointed out the influence of Mozart in the harpsichord part of George Harrison's "Little Piggies." The inclusion of a Mozart-influenced motif played on an eighteenth-century keyboard on a Beatles track intrigued me. At that particular time, I was a follower of a classically orientated band, the Nice, which had a keyboard player, Keith Emerson, who was as adept at holding Hammond organ keys down with a dagger and playing in reverse from the back of the instrument as he was at playing Bach, Sibelius, and Mussorgsky with a formal technique. The band's first album, *The Thoughts of Emerlist Davjack* (1967), contained a mixture of rearranged classical pieces and some contemporary rock songs. The band continued to include renditions of classical works on their later albums. It was their version of Leonard Bernstein's "America" from *West Side Story* (1957), however (with an introduction from Dvořák's *From the New World* Symphony [1893]) that became one of the band's first chart successes. This particular single struck me as a new genre of rock music that at once tied in with my liberal (for the time) music studies and the visceral and virtuosic nature of rock music that had already made me musically aware of the possibilities of what became known as "rock" as opposed to "pop."

The Nice went on to record Bach's *Brandenburg Concerto No. 3 in G Major* (as "Brandenburger"), Sibelius's *Karelia Suite*, and Tchaikovsky's *Pathetique* (Symphony No. 6, 3rd Movement) before Emerson left the band to form Emerson, Lake and Palmer with Greg Lake, formerly of King Crimson, and Carl Palmer, formerly of Atomic Rooster. This may further reinforce the impression that progressive rock had its principal roots in classical music, which is partially true, given that other classically trained keyboard players—such as Wakeman of Yes, Vincent Crane of Atomic Rooster, Tony Banks of Genesis, Hugh Banton of Van Der Graaf Generator, Robert John Godfrey of the Enid, and Jon Lord of Deep Purple—were all part of the progressive rock genre. One could also add John Paul Jones, the bassist and keyboard player for Led Zeppelin, to this list, given his high level of classical music education and who had indeed undergone the training normally given to those musicians intending to enter a classical career.

However, despite the inclusion of many classical references in their progressive performances, in all cases, other music—most often jazz and blues—had a profound influence (for example, Deep Purple's first hit, "Hush" [1968], had a long rhythm and blues–style Hammond organ solo). Other musicians, however, took progressive rock further.

The genre therefore emerged from a mixed perspective of single and album success in the wake of albums already mentioned. Several of the bands involved in early musical experimentation originally had been bands that had achieved success in the popular music charts. Already mentioned was the move toward conceptuality by the Beatles and the Moody Blues. Pink Floyd gradually became more progressive after Syd Barrett's departure, particularly after the release of "Dark Side of the Moon" (1973), but the Who, the Small Faces, Family, Jethro Tull, and the Kinks had single successes, sometimes while releasing progressive rock albums. On the other hand, there were progressive rock bands that formed with the express purpose of experimentation; this was the case with King Crimson, Genesis, and the combination of established musicians that became Emerson, Lake and Palmer (ELP). ELP originally wanted Jimi Hendrix's drummer Mitch Mitchell, who was unavailable for contractual reasons, and a later lineup of ELP included Cozy Powell on drums before the band reunited with Carl Palmer after a hiatus.

Other bands that had achieved earlier pop success reinvented themselves, such as the aforementioned Gentle Giant, which was formerly Simon Dupree and the Big Sound. This band had had chart success with "Kites" (1967), a song that had a Chinese flavor (perfect fourth intervals between notes like the open lower strings of a guitar played in pairs) to its harmony and instrumentation and a spoken Chinese section. It also featured the ubiquitous Mellotron.

Capability Brown, formerly Harmony Grass, was a predominantly vocal harmony band. Members had had chart successes as Tony Rivers and the Castaways before changing the band's name to Harmony Grass and releasing one album in 1969 to moderate acclaim. Some members then reformed as Capability Brown and retained their vocal harmonies but increased the complexity of band arrangements.

Argent was a band formed by the Zombies' keyboard player, Rod Argent, and guitarist Russell Ballard. Ballard, like several of his peers, had enjoyed earlier chart success with pop singer Adam Faith and the band Unit 4+2. Argent's two most successful chart entries, other than several albums, were "Hold Your Head Up" (1972), featuring a long, classically orientated and harmonically dense Hammond organ solo from Argent himself, and "God Gave Rock and Roll to You" (1973). Robin Lumley of Brand X joined a later version of the band that also featured members of Weather Report and Frank Zappa's band. Lumley described the experience: "Then after a stint producing an album for Rod Argent, I joined the Argent touring band, which included Chester

Thompson [Weather Report and Frank Zappa] and Alphonso Johnson [Weather Report]. . . . What a gas!"[5]

Dantalion's Chariot, formerly Zoot Money and the Big Roll Band, a band that originally played American rhythm and blues in the styles of Ray Charles and Fats Waller (and whose guitarist, Andy Summers, later cofounded the Police), also joined the progressive rock clique and at one time boasted a light show larger than that of Pink Floyd.[6] The band wore white clothing on stage to highlight the impact of the light show.

It was virtuosity, curiosity, visual impression, and musical eclecticism (elements that increase in number as this book progresses), that originally defined progressive rock music, and this trend has continued throughout the history of the genre. If one were to ignore the media term "progressive," however, one might call the genre "sophisticated rock," but like all music, advances in any form instigate progression, so the term stuck. This is unsurprising, given the number of musicians from so many different musical backgrounds that were involved in its inception. Whether these bands and their members had already experienced pop chart success, purposely had formed bands to experiment with musical influences learned at school and conservatoires, or had heard influences on available recordings, it is significant that record companies at the time either formed to support and promote the genre (for example, Island, Chrysalis, and Charisma, whose founder Tony Stratton-Smith said he was more interested in bands having long and successful careers than a hit single and nothing with which to follow it) or were subsidiaries of already existing major labels. These include Harvest (**EMI**) and Vertigo (Philips). The issue thus arose of how to describe a new musical style that went against the trend of three-minute pop songs.

Terms such as "classical rock," "blues rock," and "folk-rock" (as opposed to the blues and folk music played during the blues and folk revivals that had occurred in the 1950s and 1960s, in which authenticity was paramount) were in common use by the late 1960s.[7] Paul Stump maintains that "the marriage of folk and rock [for example] was always on rock music's terms" and that the term "folk-rock" was coined by various record companies, mainly Island Records, to describe one of their bands, Fairport Convention.[8] Any combination of rock music with another style encourages this kind of dual descriptor, but the issue remains, why call it "progressive"?

One possible reason is that the genre was free of any strict boundaries imposed by record companies or even audiences. Although bands of the early 1960s were under the control of producers and record companies following what is often referred to as the "British invasion" of America by U.K. bands that were successful in the United States in the wake of the Beatles' success, some British bands embraced the psychedelic counterculture that was becoming established there, especially on the West Coast.[9] Edward Macan regards the progressive bands he discusses in his comprehensive study of the style as part of a British counterculture that grew from the influence of American popular music experimentation.[10] I would extend that view to all European progressive rock at the time. The music was, and is, often referred to as "the underground," especially by the previous generation of hippies from the 1960s. In their discussions on the origins of the progressive rock style, both Macan and Richie Unterberger provide insightful narratives describing its background as in the earlier acid rock psychedelia of the mid- to late 1960s.[11] Macan acknowledges the contribution to progressive rock made by rhythm and blues, and by the late 1960s and early 1970s blues rock performers often came from a level of technical virtuosity that Macan perceives as a legacy drawn from classical music as well as from the tradition of the virtuoso as Romantic hero that was absorbed by jazz in the 1920s.[12] In his own discussion of the components of the progressive rock style, John R. Palmer states that the style predominantly drew upon Western art music referents, although this often has proved not to be the case.[13]

Macan is more expansive about progressive rock and its ephemera, describing the music as constituting a Wagnerian *Gesamkunstwerk* in which "music, visual motifs and verbal expression are inextricably intertwined to convey a coherent artistic vision."[14] Put simply and using the progressive rock LP album as an example, the experience of "listening" is only one component of the progressive rock experience. Leaving the live performance aside, purchasing a progressive album was not simply purchasing a recording. It included sophisticated artwork on, most often, a gatefold double cover (sometimes with extra pages of text inside); printed lyrics; lists of musicians, engineers, and producers involved; studios in which the album was recorded; and often other elements that enhanced the experience. Whereas the typical pop albums of the 1960s usually featured a photograph of the performer or band, progressive rock album design assisted in establishing the genre in a new era, and the cover art was as important as the music it contained, *Sgt. Pepper* being an early example. The issue of a reinvented concept of audience reception of recorded music is discussed in the next chapter.

A TECHNOLOGICAL NOTE ON THE "PROGRESSIVE" SOUNDSCAPE

Musical virtuosity, stylistic eclecticism, and even sartorial fashion had profound effects on the emergence of progressive rock, although one must acknowledge that the late 1960s and early 1970s was a period of technological advances in how music was performed and recorded. This issue is discussed further in a later chapter, but there was one particular instrument that was already in use in studios in the mid-1960s that was already being used by established performers. The Mellotron became almost a trademark sound for several progressive rock bands, and many have used this keyboard since the inception of the genre in the late 1960s. (The latest version at the time of this writing is the comparatively smaller and lighter digital Mellotron 4000D.) The bands using early Mellotrons in live performance included the Moody Blues and the Graham Bond Organisation, though the instrument was originally intended for studio, not live, performance. Originally a U.S. invention by Harry Chamberlin, the Mellotron was built in the United Kingdom in 1963. It was a large double manual (two keyboards alongside each other) instrument that contained multiple spools of prerecorded sounds on tape that could be played in the same manner as the familiar piano-style keyboard. Until this point, most bands with keyboard players used keyboards such as Vox Continental organs (notably the Animals on "The House of the Rising Sun"), Wurlitzer pianos, Fender Rhodes pianos, RMI pianos, and, when affordable, Hammond organs. The original Moog synthesizer, a large and complex array of modules and connecting cables much like a telephone exchange, had already been used on many successful albums of the time, but it was impractical to use outside the recording studio, given its size and delicacy. The same could be said about the early Mellotrons, which featured standard sounds such as woodwinds, strings, and voices, all delicately mounted on small tape spools. In addition to the Moody Blues, the Beatles used the Mellotron on many of their later recordings (for example "Strawberry Fields Forever" [1967] and *Abbey Road* [1969]). In the early 1960s, each Mellotron cost about £1,000 ($1,319 US); average British house prices at the time were between £2,000 ($2,637 US) and £3,000 ($3,956 US). It weighed 160 kilograms (353 pounds). In 1969, the Mellotron manufacturers produced the second generation MKII instrument, which was cheaper, lighter, and more durable. This model became popular following King Crimson's seminal first album, *In the Court of the Crimson King* (1969).

SUMMONING BACK THE FIRE WITCH

King Crimson used the newly developed MKII Mellotron keyboard in live settings as well as in the studio, giving the band an ethereal sound that many other progressive rock bands later copied. Arguably, King Crimson was one of the first bands labelled "progressive," and they presented "performance" as a visual as well as an aural experience. The band was one of the few progressive rock bands of the time that featured its own light show (as opposed to lighting supplied by a venue), thus supporting a view that progressive rock performances and recordings were not simply gigs or albums to be listened to as background music for their audiences. At King Crimson performances, colored lights were projected onto the band by the band's principal lyricist, Peter Sinfield, rather than using the familiar follow spotlights and overhead lighting. This practice was reminiscent of the psychedelic light shows that were regular features at rock concerts in the United States and were arguably influenced by Joe's Lights, an innovative group of U.S. lighting technicians who used a back projection made by light shining through rotating glass slides containing hot, colored oils. The effect was a collage of swirling color that also highlighted the musicians on whom it was projected and possibly a reason why there is a fine line between definitions of late psychedelia and early progressive rock.

Using an instrumental lineup of drums, electric and acoustic guitars, vibraphone, and various woodwind instruments, the addition of the often otherworldly quality of the Mellotron made King Crimson's sonic identity stand out from other bands using more standard instrumentation. To put the band's sonic status in progressive rock in the late 1960s and early 1970s in context, one must also add the other keyboard technologies available for live progressive rock performance, such as the newly introduced Minimoog, a monophonic but portable Moog synthesizer, and the Hammond organ, instruments that became familiar in the progressive rock instrumental panoply. However, the Mellotron's limitation of note length was not a problem for King Crimson, even though the keyboard player could hold a note for only around eleven seconds before having to release the key so that the tape spool could rewind. The band thus used only one keyboard in its early stages. The Mellotron is featured to great effect on most tracks on the album, most notably "Epitaph" and the title track, "In the Court of the Crimson King." One must also acknowledge that this album featured the band members' instrumental virtuosity—Robert Fripp's jazz influences and use of early guitar processing technologies; Ian McDonald's performance of wind, keyboard instruments, and vibraphone; Greg Lake's bass guitar, acoustic guitar, and lead vocals; and Mike Giles's jazz-influenced drumming. The opening track, "21st-Century Schizoid Man," features an improvised six-beat jazz/swing section before returning to the apocalyptic lyrics with Lake's voice processed for distortion. "Epitaph," and "In the Court of the Crimson King," also contain dark, apocalyptic messages. Though the contemplative lyrics of the penultimate track, "Moonchild," draw on typical hippy whimsy of the time, the dark content of the other two tracks are worthy of further examination. Both draw on a sense of gathering pre- or postwar gloom, arguably reflective of the political situations of the time (the cold war, nuclear threats, etc.), with lyrics concerning sunlight shining on instruments of death and the lack of movement toward peace as silence drowns opposition. These lyrics echo the works written about the silence that followed the end of World War I, when public opinion wanted to put finality to the episode.[15] Other lyrics predict the end of humanity and include the "Black Queen" chanting "the funeral march to summon back the fire witch" to the court of the Crimson King.

To place an all-encompassing definition on the band thus proves difficult as the music and lyrics move from jazz, rock, and the avant-garde in music and poetry of the time. "Moonchild" has a long, gentle improvised section (twelve minutes) that segues into the darkness of the title track, leaving the listener lulled into a dreamlike security that is shattered by the gravity of the title track's lyrical message. The message is reinforced by the combination of rock guitar and Mellotron in the mix. The band's initial reputation was firmly established by its performance at the Rolling Stones concert commemorating Brian Jones's death in 1969. Unfortunately, this lineup lasted for only this album. Lake left to join Emerson, Lake and Palmer, and other members started their own projects, leaving Fripp to form what would become the first of several iconic lineups that featured some of the finest progressive rock musicians. It must also be added that King Crimson are still performing in the new millennium and remain a major influence on many of the more recent progressive-oriented bands such as Tool, a band King Crimson supported on a U.S. tour in 2002. Tool found this situation rather intimidating, and Michael James Keenan of Tool expressed the band's respect for King Crimson: "Robert Fripp said he had been writing a lot of heavier songs in response to what he's heard from us. . . . [It's] terrifying to have him go out and open for us, because he's the master. We've always copped to being influenced by Crimson and to have them play ahead of us. . . . I'm afraid that the kids are going to hear Crimson and say 'Tool ripped these songs off.'" [16]

Tool certainly follow progressive tropes. A recommended album is the seventy-nine minute, suite-like recording *Lateralus* (2001), which is sung in an invented language, was rereleased with a gatefold cover in 2005, and, like many songs from earlier progressive bands, encourages humanity to explore a deeper understanding of itself and its world. The band also uses irregular meters on the album (another progressive trope—9/8, 8/8, and 7/8—in keeping with mathematical structures such as the Fibonacci sequence, a compositional and musicological equation beyond the scope of this study). The album was certified double platinum in 2003.

King Crimson's musical legacy is apparent among the later progressive rock bands, and this is discussed in later chapters.

ROCK MEETS JAZZ AND BLUES

Another album from the early period of progressive rock that demands serious attention from listeners investigating the genre is *Valentyne Suite* (1969) by Colosseum. *Valentyne Suite* was Colosseum's second album, the first being *Those Who Are about to Die Salute You* (1969).

Founding members of Colosseum—drummer Jon Hiseman, tenor saxo-phonist Dick Heckstall-Smith, and bassist Tony Reeves—had, like many other successful 1960s musicians, originally been part of the 1960s blues revival and had performed with British blues legends John Mayall and Graham Bond (Eric Clapton, Peter Green, John McVie, Mick Fleetwood, and Jack Bruce being a few other examples). Colos-seum added Dave Greenslade on Hammond organ, an instrument in-vented in the 1930s in the United States for use in churches that did not have a pipe organ but that soon became popular with jazz and blues musicians, eventually becoming a mainstay in progressive rock. The Hammond organ lacked the ethereal nature of the Mellotron but added both a gritty blues sound and a rich church-like tone to progressive rock's many variations. Having said that, jazz and classically oriented progressive styles utilized the versatility provided by the Leslie rotating speaker cabinet, which characterizes the Hammond organ sound.

Jim Roche was Colosseum's original guitarist but soon was replaced by James Litherland, who in turn was replaced by Clem Clempson for the band's third album, *Daughter of Time* (1970). Hiseman then added Chris Farlowe, already a successful soul singer, as a vocalist. The lineup continued to be fluid with bassists, then finally with Mark Clarke, who joined in 1970. Again, John Peel was influential in the initial growth in the band's popularity, but, as with King Crimson, the band membership wasn't initially stable. Colosseum of that period can be situated at the jazz end of the progressive spectrum. Unlike Miles Davis's use of guitar (with guitarist John McLaughlin) on *Bitches Brew* (1970), Colosseum's sound was more rock and blues oriented with jazz overtones and more guitar driven, even with the jazz-oriented soloing of Heckstall-Smith and the rhythm and blues of Greenslade's keyboards. Clempson drew on a broad range of influences, and Hiseman's drumming roots were in the jazz of the 1950s and 1960s. Colosseum thus paralleled the jazz-rock fusion bands that were emerging in the United States (Chicago Transit Authority, Blood Sweat and Tears, and, later in the 1970s, Re-turn to Forever, Weather Report, and others). In the United Kingdom, If, Caravan, Egg, Patto, Tempest, Hatfield the North, Ian Carr's Nu-cleus, Isotope, and Soft Machine (and their many spinoffs as musicians joined other bands or formed new ones) are a few examples of the same jazz stylistic direction taken within U.K. progressive rock. Many of these bands' musicians became a part of what was referred to in the

1980s as "Eurojazz," part of the jazz-rock fusion genres that comprised jazz and jazz-rock musicians from all of Europe.

In the 1970s, Colosseum recorded three studio albums and one double live album, *Colosseum Live* (1971). The band was signed to Vertigo Records, a Philips subsidiary that specialized in progressive rock, one of several formed by major labels to specialize in progressive rock. Following the band's initial success, Colosseum disbanded, and members had varying degrees of success with other projects, principally Clempson, who replaced Peter Frampton in Humble Pie. The longest period the band spent together was a reunion between 1994 to 2015 with a lineup of Hiseman, Clempson, Heckstall-Smith (who died in 2004 and was replaced by saxophonist Barbara Thompson, Hiseman's wife), Farlowe, Greenslade, and Clarke. Progressive rock reunions are discussed in a later chapter.

"Valentyne Suite Three: The Grass Is Always Greener" is the final track on *Valentyne Suite*. It is a song built from one central scale and has a Spanish tonality, while also drawing on blues and jazz, typical eclecticism of progressive rock. It is largely constructed from a scale that many composers have used to create an exotic Spanish feel to their music, a modal scale called "Phrygian" (find E on a keyboard and then play the seven white notes that follow it). The entire song is constructed from chords built on each step of this scale. The track opens with the whole band playing a combination of these notes as a type of fanfare that lasts sixteen measures before punctuating the extended solo section with fast saxophone riffs played by Heckstall-Smith (who was able to play soprano and tenor saxophones simultaneously), doubled with Greenslade's keyboards and Litherland's guitar. The solos follow the chord sequence of the main melodic section of the song.

All of these chords are linked by notes from the Spanish inflections of the Phrygian scale. The solos that follow mostly use one round of this chord cycle: first, a Hammond organ solo, which is followed by the fast saxophone-led riff. A bass solo (actually two basses double-tracked in harmony with each other) and finally the guitar solo over six rounds of the cycle doubles the tempo of the piece before the band changes to a free-form, sustained drone and then returns to the original melodic theme and the fanfare-like section that opened the tune. The piece is almost seven minutes long and another example of the freedom of track length that progressive rock bands enjoyed. There's a live version of this track recorded in 1994 at one of the band's first reunion concerts on *Live Cologne 1994* featuring Hiseman, Heckstall-Smith, Clempson, Greenslade, and Clarke.[17] Since it is an instrumental, Farlowe is not featured but can be seen briefly at the right of the stage. The audience reaction to the band's 1994 performance of "The Grass Is Always Greener," particularly Clempson's guitar solo, is ecstatic.

MOUNTAINS COME OUT OF THE SKY

A third example of progressive rock in its early stages is "Roundabout" by Yes. On the band's fourth album, *Fragile* (1971), the track was released at a time when the band already had established itself as one of the most significant and popular progressive rock acts.

Originally called Mabel Greer's Toyshop in 1967, the band was reformed in 1968 by bassist Chris Squire and singer Jon Anderson. They were joined by their former band members, guitarist Peter Banks, keyboard player Tony Kaye, and drummer Bill Bruford. Like many other bands of the period, each member was experienced from playing in several other bands performing on the London rock circuit. Various fortuitous introductions led to the formation of this lineup, and despite the many important performances the band played in its initial rise to success (including supporting Cream at that band's final concert), their first televised performance was a U.K. children's television program called *Magpie* in 1969. Despite being a children's program, the show's theme song was performed by the rhythm and blues–based Spencer Davis Group, and it was regarded by many children and teenagers as a more credible alternative to the BBC's flagship yet staid children's program, *Blue Peter*. Thus, Yes gained an early fan base among young people who would become the student-based audience that followed them in later years.

Yes' first two albums were well received by fans and critics and contained several songs by other songwriters, including the Beatles. The band's second album, *Time and a Word* (1970), used an orchestra and contains references to the score from the film *The Big Country* (1958), composed by Jerome Moross, and to Gustav Holst's "Jupiter" from the *Planets Suite* (1916). It was their third album, *The Yes Album* (1971) that reached number four in the United Kingdom and number forty in the United States. This album solidified Yes' reputation among progress rock bands such as King Crimson, and both bands became benchmarks for musicianship and musical creativity in progressive rock. Other bands also established reputations for the same reasons (Gentle Giant, Focus, and Jethro Tull are examples, but, as stated in the introduction, this book is not intended as a comprehensive history of progressive rock).

Like many other progressive rock bands, cracks in personal relationships appeared as success increased. Peter Banks was replaced for *The Yes Album* by Steve Howe, who had previously been in a band called Keith West's Tomorrow and had played on "Excerpt from a Teenage Opera" (1967), which achieved chart success in the United Kingdom. I first saw Steve Howe perform when he was in Tomorrow in 1969 at the Royal Albert Hall supporting Eric Clapton with Delaney and Bonnie and Friends. Howe's expert musicianship was apparent in comparison to the rest of the band and, apart from playing a jazz-orientated electric guitar (a Gibson ES175, which was unusual in a rock context), he was adept at many guitar styles not used by most blues-influenced guitarists of the time.

By the time Yes released *Fragile* in 1971, the band had replaced keyboard player Kaye with session musician Rick Wakeman, who had studied at the Royal College of Music and had been a member of the Strawbs. He also had recorded with David Bowie, T. Rex, and Elton John. Though the music magazine *Melody Maker* reported that Kaye's departure was due to his unwillingness to use new keyboard technologies, such as the Mellotron and the Minimoog, Yes were quick to point out Wakeman's versatility on piano, Hammond organ, Mellotron, and Minimoog, thus Wakeman became Yes' foil to Keith Emerson of Emerson, Lake and Palmer; Jon Lord of Deep Purple; and Tony Banks of Genesis, all of whom had similar abilities and came from classical backgrounds.

The album *Fragile* has several band tracks, but it also features solo tracks from various members of the band. Wakeman's was a synthesizer version of an excerpt from Brahms's *Symphony No. 4 in E Minor*, which he renamed "Cans and Brahms." A prominent track on *Fragile* is "Roundabout." The piece features the entire band but starts with an acoustic guitar introduction played solo by Howe, followed by a fast, driving bass line on which Squire used his trademark bass, the Rickenbacker 4001, a stereo bass guitar which had a "dry" channel (the usual sound of the bass) and another channel that used overdrive (distortion as well as other studio effects). Critics of progressive rock regard Squire's bass lines as "busy" or "crowded," but his bass line on "Roundabout" has become an iconic, "semi–lead guitar" line among progressive bassists, for whom its performance became a rite of passage in learning progressive rock performance in the 1970s. The combination of Squire's driving bass line and Bruford's jazz-influenced drums complements each other, despite the rhythmic complexity of both. As with many Yes songs (or, for that matter, many progressive rock songs), "Roundabout" contains many "irregular meter" measures (i.e., measures that do not contain the standard divisions of four beats common to most pop songs). The band switches between measures of four, three, and six beats throughout the song. Although there are three distinct parts to the song, none accurately can be termed a chorus. The third section, probably the most rock oriented, does contain a solid pulse when compared to the rest of the song, yet it is constructed from repeated sections of three four-beat measures followed by a two-beat grouping. Most significantly, Wakeman uses his Hammond to play a Bach-influenced motif over the whole section. Wakeman often drew on his classical training on later Yes albums and his solo work.

Yes became a progressive rock influence for many bands whose success occurred later in the 1970s, the Canadian band Rush and the U.S. band Dream Theater being examples.[18] Peter Banks's own band, Flash, which he formed after his departure from Yes, was also influenced by his former band. Anderson's vocal style is another feature of Yes that contributes to the band's unique sound. His high tenor voice coupled with Squire's high register voice for the harmonies he sang provides a rich vocal blend that few bands have emulated successfully. While Geddy Lee, the lead vocalist and bassist of Rush, also possesses a wide vocal register, his voice lacks the richness that Anderson uses to great effect. One thing that Yes and Rush have in common is the illusory and fantasy-like nature of the content of their lyrics. Whereas Neil Peart, the Rush drummer, writes most of his band's lyrics, Anderson is the main lyricist for Yes. Again, as with some King Crimson lyrics, hippy whimsy is apparent in most Yes songs. Lyrics contain what seem to be references to a fantasy world that has been influential to their album artwork from *Fragile* onward, such as "mountains coming out of the sky" (from

"And You and I") and "crossing the shapes of the morning" to "reach over the sun for the river" (from "Roundabout"). These whimsical lyrics were accentuated in album sleeve artwork created by Roger Dean.

The existential content of "And You and I" carries a dream-like quality that can be interpreted in many ways, from being a love song to a drug experience, another progressive rock trait. It also purposely avoids the standard verse/chorus structure of most pop music. Anderson states that he originally wrote the main body of the song in conjunction with Howe, intending it to be a folk song.[19] However, the complexity of the arrangement gradually increased, which is why it is also credited to the other band members.

A significant issue that becomes apparent in progressive rock is the willing fluidity of membership in many of the bands that were successful during the 1970s and the 1980s. Although some members left bands and did not continue their musical careers, many progressive bands seemed to rotate their musicians. For example, Bruford left Yes to join King Crimson, which at that time also featured John Wetton, a bassist who had already been in Mogul Thrash and Family and who had worked with several members of previous lineups of King Crimson and Bryan Ferry. Wetton later formed Asia with Steve Howe, Carl Palmer (of ELP), and Geoff Downes (a later member of Yes). This kind of musical camaraderie, outside personal conflict that often occurs across all kinds of music, is particularly apparent in progressive rock, and it has led to many new bands made up of personnel from other bands, which has created even more fusions of musical styles.

THE FIRST PROGRESSIVE ROCK "SUPERGROUP"

It is significant that when Emerson, Lake and Palmer left their earlier bands and formed what might be regarded as the first progressive rock supergroup in 1970, their production aesthetic was to combine their musicianship with a visual experience (including onstage cannons) that would make them a leading band in the genre. Their album covers were created by leading designers and artists such as Storm Thorgerson, who also created iconic artwork for Pink Floyd, and H. R. Giger, who created figures for the *Alien* films.

Emerson's knowledge of classical music combined with the rhythm-section intricacies of both Lake and Palmer was lauded from the band's first performances, including a front-page review in *Melody Maker* (despite the band's desire to start their performances playing in small venues). Before the band signed to Atlantic Records, they regularly filled stadia, although it was the band's performance at the Isle of Wight Festival in August 1970 that firmly established their reputation. Emerson continued to demonstrate his classical virtuosity and performed the music in an aggressive visual style that at once showed his respect for his choice of repertoire, while using the aforementioned Nazi daggers wedged between his Hammond organ keys to hold down notes. These daggers were thrown at his Leslie cabinets when not in use. He also balanced his Hammond on his legs while playing effortlessly from behind the instrument. Bear in mind that the weight of a Hammond organ in the 1970s was quite considerable, but Emerson also balanced it on its side while playing it. Thus, the visual aspects of Emerson, Lake and Palmer matched the eclecticism of their combination of existing classical music and original material. Classical music performed and recorded was most often adapted for rock performance and rarely played as the composer intended. Examples are "The Barbarian" (based of Béla Bartók's *Allegro barbaro*) and Copland's *Fanfare for the Common Man* (Copland gave his permission to the band for the recording).

These are only two examples of many, but Atlantic Records was wary about the band recording and releasing Mussorgsky's *Pictures at an Exhibition* (1874), as they gradually started to attract criticism from rock critics such as Robert Christgau, who stated, "The pomposities of *Tarkus* [the band's second album recorded in 1971] and the monstrosities of the Mussorgsky homage clinch it—these guys are as stupid as their most pretentious fans."[20] Even John Peel had become critical of what had become an excessive stage show that included Lake performing on a Persian carpet, Palmer's stainless steel drum kit, and Emerson's increasing number of keyboards, describing the band as "a waste of talent and electricity."[21] ELP attracted criticism such as this from many quarters, but the band was a product of its own success at a time when ticket prices matched the scale of the event the audience wished to see. Criticism of excessive performance aesthetics aside, the band's own compositions, the virtuosity with which they are played, and the band's awareness of technological advances are all worthy of attention.

Rather than discussing the band's earlier recordings, I have purposely chosen to examine one of their later recordings released in the 1990s. "Black Moon," the title track from an Emerson, Lake and Palmer album that was recorded in 1992, demonstrates the band's determination to contemporize their sound. Although the album was criticized for not being to the standard of the earlier *Brain Salad Surgery* (1973), the instrumental sounds used in the song reflect that the individual band members retained their musical abilities and their curiosity for the latest technologies, given that the production aesthetic is current for the period, although even the use of contemporary technologies fails to impress Paul Stump on the grounds of "some quite horrid keyboard sounds" but who also adds that "there was a vigour" in the band's live performances.[22] I programmed Lake's effect racks prior to the tour that promoted the album, and the range of equipment used by all members for live performance was state of the art for its time because the band intended to sound contemporary rather than rework their earlier sonic successes.

Despite earlier criticisms for being pretentious and overblown in live performance, the band retained their reputation for using sound reinforcement and lighting. Lake's Persian rug was laid in front of his amplification and he read lyrics from an autocue system normally used for television newsreaders. His amplification system consisted of 3,600 watts of power amplifiers contained in six large flight cases along with his effect units. Emerson had a range of digital keyboards, as well as his original Moog synthesizer system and a Hammond organ. Palmer had a double bass drum kit with many tom-toms that were held by a frame surrounding the kit. Unusually, there were no microphones on the kit. Instead, each drum had a sensor attached to it that fed acoustic drum sounds into two large sampling units, which contained prerecorded sounds from dozens of drum kits that Palmer could change with the use of foot pedals. Thus, the band had aided reinvention of itself by using the latest technological advances in instrumentation and amplification. The lighting system was also extremely large and used the latest technologies to highlight each member of the band. In other words, Emerson, Lake and Palmer were determined to maintain their use of contemporary technologies for which they had once been criticized. The music had changed—it was still complex—but with a 1990s style that retained virtuosity while moving away from their previous organ, bass guitar, and drums instrumentation.

"Black Moon" starts with a pounding, almost heavy metal riff punctuated by bass riffs from a synthesizer and orchestral sound "stabs" (very short, percussive chords) from a keyboard sampler. The processed, reverberating drum sound is used to emulate a similar drum pattern as that used by Queen on "Radio Gaga" and an obvious means by which the band would get its audience to engage in clapping to the repetitive rhythm in live performances. However, unlike Queen's pop rock hit, "Black Moon" then moves in typical progressive rock style into a lighter section at three minutes, twenty-two seconds (the entire track is six minutes, fifty-eight seconds long) that takes on an almost hurdy-gurdy-like folk sound. This precedes a return to the main pounding riff and enables Emerson to play a short solo that demonstrates his ability to use his keyboards as a small orchestra. There is a similar section at five minutes when a flutelike solo develops into a counterpoint (several melodies played simultaneously in harmony). The bass line then moves away from the main riff and plays a continually ascending line in harmony with the melodies being played on various keyboards. The song ends with echoes of the earlier Emerson, Lake and Palmer. Emerson plays a short Hammond organ solo over a return to the principal riff.

The lyrical content of "Black Moon" bears a distinct similarity to the lyrics Lake sang on "In the Court of the Crimson King." There is a dark, pre-apocalyptic message that forewarns a bleak future. The use of lyrics that portray futuristic and fantastical imagery with dark messages or with whimsical, literary descriptions, quickly became commonplace in progressive rock (for example, "Supper's Ready" by Genesis, which is discussed in the next chapter). This defining factor has continued until the present and can be heard on many Scandinavian progressive rock albums that draw on dark Nordic legends for influences.

Throughout Emerson, Lake and Palmer's career, the band often utilized Lake's ability to sing and play acoustic guitar (as he had previously done in King Crimson), and an example of this very different sound can be heard on the much earlier "Lucky Man," which was recorded in 1970. During songs such as this, Emerson played bass lines on a keyboard, providing extra sonic texture for the band.

It would seem, therefore, that bands such as ELP were still popular enough to break established pop music boundaries while also attracting audiences to large stadia in the 1990s. Band longevity is another significant defining feature of progressive rock, along with virtuosity and freedom to experiment with the combination of multiple musical styles and technologies.

JAZZ-BASED BLUES TO FOLK AND ROCK

Another album that breaks the accepted boundaries set by the pop music industry is *Aqualung* (1971) by Jethro Tull. One of the few progressive rock bands to enjoy earlier chart success, Jethro Tull had been successful in the international charts with "Living in the Past" (1969). This song was unusual, as it is constructed with five beats in each measure, unlike most pop music of the time, which had four beats per measure. Other exceptions to audience familiarity with four-beat measures are Paul Desmond's "Take Five" (performed by the Dave Brubeck Quartet [1959]) and Pink Floyd's "Money" (1973) (combining seven-beat measures with four-beat measures).

Aqualung was Jethro Tull's fourth album. There had been some changes to the initial lineup. The original guitarist, Mick Abrahams, left due to the band's gradual move away from jazz-based blues (as on the band's first album, *This Was* [1968]). He was replaced by Martin Barre. The band also added Jeffrey Hammond on bass in place of the original bassist, Glenn Cornick (who played on parts of *Aqualung* and then formed his own band, Wild Turkey, a common occurrence in early progressive rock, in which band members often left between or during albums and then formed a new band. Indeed, Mick Abrahams formed Blodwyn Pig, a blues rock band, after his tenure in Jethro Tull). Jethro Tull originally had four members, but by 1971 John Evan had joined on piano, Hammond organ, and Mellotron.

Jethro Tull started to experiment with a combination of extended songs that drew upon a fusion of styles such as jazz, folk, and heavy, powerful riffs that bordered on what had become known as heavy metal. "Aqualung," the title track, was written by lead vocalist and multi-instrumentalist Ian Anderson and his wife, Jennie. It was inspired by photographs she had taken of homeless people forced to live on the embankment of the Thames. Though the band always denied that *Aqualung* was a concept album, there are lyrical links between songs concerning the human suffering depicted in the photographs and Anderson's views on religion. These links between songs are a common theme that defines progressive rock in terms of conceptuality and complexity of arrangement. An example is "Cross-eyed Mary," the song immediately following "Aqualung," which tells the story of a teenage prostitute who is attracted to older men. The character described in "Aqualung" is mentioned in the lyrics of "Cross-eyed Mary."

"Aqualung" is six minutes, thirty-five seconds long and has four distinct sections. It starts with a heavy metal riff that is dissonant (notes that are not connected to a particular key and that cause a sense of unease to the listener), reflecting the pitiful condition of the character in the song.

The first section is broken up by two-beat measures every four bars, further supporting the lyrics in the opening section that describe the state of the central character, who is obviously homeless and watching children play, perhaps with evil intent. This opening lyric is descriptive and almost critical of the character, but the next section breaks down to a solo acoustic guitar (played by Anderson) that opens the second section of five sung verses that address the character with pity and the promise of a cup of tea from the Salvation Army, as well as what seems like a promise of support and friendship.

Throughout the verses that follow, the rest of the band gradually joins the acoustic guitar. First, the bass guitar plays an almost "walking" (jazzlike) line and is then joined by drums and piano in the third verse. In verse four, the band plays a funkier "feel" or groove that is quite sparse for the piano, bass, and drums, when compared to later sections of the song. Meanwhile, the acoustic guitar plays a double tempo rhythm across this rhythm section pattern for eighteen measures. At this point, the band returns to the previous "walking" rhythm that precedes the fifth and final verse. There follows a half time (half the speed of the previous verses) fourteen-measure section that features the beginning of Martin Barre's guitar solo. The band then returns to the original tempo for a thirty-six-bar guitar solo over the verse chord and rhythm structure. At the end of the guitar solo, the solo acoustic guitar returns for nine measures with the first verse sung before the song's opening section of two- and four-beat measures is repeated as a finale. As with "Black Moon," there are several distinct components to "Aqualung" and the song fits any definition of progressive rock that is based on complexity of arrangement.

Jethro Tull's following album, *Thick As a Brick* (1972), took another step toward conceptuality, complex musical arrangements, and satirical humor, moving the band even further from their earlier jazz blues origins and making them a defining progressive rock band.

AN EDUCATED GUESS

A successful progressive rock band formed at a university was Van Der Graaf Generator. Songwriters Peter Hammill and Chris Judge-Smith decided to form a band while attending Manchester University in 1967. The lineup went through several changes in membership and several breakups (typical for the emerging genre) before settling into a stable lineup after signing with Charisma Records in 1969. By this time, Smith had left, and the band had contractual problems with Mercury Records, although they were resolved by Tony Stratton-Smith, the founder and owner of Charisma Records, who finally signed Hammill (who had been recording for the label as a solo artist), along with a classically trained organist, Hugh Banton, drummer Guy Evans, Nic Potter on bass, and David Jackson, a saxophonist who, like Dick Heckstall-Smith of Colosseum, could play multiple saxophones, sometimes in pairs. The band, like most of their peers in progressive rock at the time, experimented with the latest sound-processing technologies to develop their own identity. Another means of establishing the band's identity was Hammill's decision to sing with a pronounced English accent (much like Peter Gabriel) rather than a transatlantic one. Van Der Graaf Generator released its first album, *The Aerosol Grey Machine* (1969), on Mercury Records (with Potter's predecessor, Keith Ellis, on bass). The band performed regularly on John Peel's *Top Gear* radio program and joined the rock circuit of progressive rock clubs in and around London, such as the Marquee and Friar's Club, as well as the U.K. university student union circuit.

Once free from Mercury's contract, the band released its second album on Charisma (Charisma Record's first album release) in 1969. *The Least We Can Do Is Wave to Each Other* was the band's first commercial success, and Potter now had joined on bass (Ellis had left due to contractual problems with another band he had joined during one of Van Der Graaf Generator's hiatuses), Banton had changed from a Farfisa organ to an electronically modified Hammond organ, and Jackson became increasingly experimental with his customized saxophones that he processed with effect pedals designed for guitars.

The following album was *H to He Who Am the Only One* (1970). By this time, the band had become even more experimental, bordering on jazz fusion, and Potter did not feel that this direction was right for him. He played on three tracks and left. Banton played bass guitar on the rest of the album and used the bass pedals of the Hammond organ to replace the sound of bass guitar in live performance. This four-piece lineup remained stable until 1972, when they toured with label mates Genesis and Lindisfarne. Robert Fripp of King Crimson had played on a track on *H to He*, an appearance further illustrating the fluidity of progressive rock bands at this time and the collaborations that occurred when all that was needed was an acknowledgment of the performer's own label on the album sleeve credits.

Although this book does not provide a comprehensive history of the progressive genre, it is worth noting that Van Der Graff Generator had two reunions, one in 1975 and one in 2005, which is ongoing. Jackson left the band in 2007 and the remaining three members continue to record and tour as a trio. Van Der Graaf Generator released albums in 2008, 2012, and 2015.

The Least We Can Do Is Wave to Each Other from 1969 contains the track "White Hammer." The song's lyrics demonstrate Hammill's fascination with the gothic (he also enjoyed science fiction) and concerns "The Hammer of Evil" (*Malleus Maleficarum* [1487]), a reference to a publication written as a guide for witch hunters in the fifteenth century (known as *Hexenhammer* in Germany). The book was written by Dominican inquisitors of the Catholic Church, which subsequently banned it. Between the fifteenth and sixteenth centuries, however, it was reprinted thirteen times and it spread throughout Europe as a means of identifying witches.[23]

"White Hammer" starts with the Hammond organ using the slow speed of its Leslie cabinet rotor, providing an almost cathedral-like atmosphere to Hammill's lyrics. The lyrics start almost as a history lesson, although Hammill sings that the *Malleus* first appeared in 1486, which was actually the year in which it was written. It was printed in

Latin on Johannes Gutenberg's (1398–1468) recently invented printing press in 1487. Hamill goes on to say that the book was written as a means of ridding the world of witchcraft and putting the pope's fear of witches to rest. This whole section features Banton's solo cathedral-like Hammond and Hammill's vocals. He also mentions that torture methods were prescribed "to kill the black arts" described in the book. By this time, the song has turned toward rock with the entry of the bass and drums. Banton's playing becomes riff based rather than the previous hymn-like chordal arrangement.

In the third section, the band returns to the earlier slow tempo, though the bass guitar accompanies the Hammond organ. Hammill sings about the innocent people who were tortured and lost their lives due to the book's misinterpretation by religious inquisitors. After this, Van Der Graaf Generator change to a bridge section in a new key with accompaniment from the Hammond organ and bass while Hammill sings about "white" witchcraft, stating that for every witch killed, two were hidden by sympathizers. This is sung in another of the alternating rock sections. There follows a brief, requiem-like organ section before the final vocal verse, telling the listener that after two centuries of witch hunting, authorities realized that the book was worthless and although the black arts still exist, they are overpowered by "the white hammer of love." This section is accompanied by a solo cornet played by session musician Gerry Salisbury.

The song then goes through several key changes while Banton plays an organ solo, followed by a jazz-influenced solo from the saxophone. By this point, the song has become funky (more syncopated and rocklike) as it slowly breaks down for the final section, a repeated, synthesized, distorted riff that has overdubbed free-form (using a random selection of notes and sounds) saxophone solos over it. With the drums adding to the chaotic ending, the song stops abruptly at eight minutes, sixteen seconds.

Having examined six very different progressive rock bands, the question remains: why call this genre of rock music "progressive"? I suggest that the six songs analyzed here feature aspects such as virtuosity, complex arrangements, sections that do not comply with traditional notions of harmony, wide ranges of sonic dynamics, various uneven meters, and the use of newly available technologies, some of which were not intended for the instrument on which they were used. Such songs that did not conform to the earlier model of a pop song broke and continue to break musical boundaries, thus progression allows the music to reach new and continually changing areas of music. The next chapter examines how advances in recording technologies, instrumentation, and means of amplification enabled progressive rock bands to adopt the methods used by classical composers—to whom the length of a piece of music was not an issue. The long-playing record enabled progressive rock compositions to extend even further in length. Also, the new progressive musical complexities could be reproduced in live contexts, a development acknowledged by all of my interviewees and other contributing informants.

2

CONCEPTUALITY

Embracing the Long Player and Technology Advances in
Sound Reproduction

TECHNOLOGY AND THE INCEPTION OF
PROGRESSIVE ROCK

The twelve-inch "long player" (LP) vinyl disc (which rotates at 33 rpm) was introduced in 1948, the seven-inch vinyl disc (45 rpm) for "single" songs and extended play (EP), with up to four tracks, followed in 1949. LPs could contain about twenty minutes of music on each side; however, their popularity was not established in pop music until the early 1960s.[1] Prior to these technical developments, recorded music had been distributed on 78-rpm shellac discs since the 1920s (although the laterally recorded disc had been invented by Emile Berliner in the late nineteenth century) as they gradually replaced phonographic cylinders. Though the shellac disc contained more recording space than the cylinder, it still had time limitations in that each side contained only three to four minutes of music. Most recordings of the first part of the twentieth century, apart from the limited availability of jazz, blues, and ragtime, were of classical music.[2] These recordings included symphonies and operas and were purchased as a collection of 78-rpm discs (the original "boxed set"). The listener, therefore, had the inconvenience of changing the disc every three or four minutes during an extended piece of music. With the emergence of the LP, many of these early 78-rpm

classical recordings were transferred to the new media, often laborious-
ly, as in the case of Wagner's Ring Cycle, which required the fadeouts
occurring at the end of each 78-rpm disc to be masked for the sake of
apparent continuity.[3]

The possibility of twenty minutes of music on each side of a vinyl LP
made a departure from an established recording format used by pop
bands, such as those described in this chapter and chapter 1. As described in chapter 1, however, progressive bands had record company
support in the composition of extended pieces of music.[4] Though not
unusual in classical music, the notion of one continuous piece of progressive rock music lasting a whole side of a long-playing vinyl disc
became the norm. For example, Genesis' "Supper's Ready" on *Foxtrot*
(1972) was twenty-two minutes long, Yes' *Tales from Topographic
Oceans* (1973), a double-disc album, contained one continuous track on
each of its four sides, and Yes' live album *Yessongs* (1973) was a triple-
disc set that contained almost two hours of the band's music performed
live in concert. The length of the tracks was, however, starting to garner
negative criticism from some fans and the music press on the basis of
self-indulgence and lack of cohesion.[5] This issue is discussed further in
the next chapter.

As previously stated, although *Sgt. Pepper* might be regarded as the
first "concept" album, there exists a progression in the Beatles' albums
from *Rubber Soul* (1965) and *Revolver* (1966) onward, especially in
terms of the sophistication of songwriting techniques, studio performance abilities, and use of studio technologies that were emerging at
the time.[6] This progression is also supported by all of my informants,
both for this study and in general conversations during our professional
careers. By the time the Beatles released *Sgt. Pepper* in 1967, however,
the songs and their order on the long-playing record had taken on a
conceptual nature in which there was a thematic connection throughout
the album.[7] The album itself was originally intended to be a collection
of songs about the band's native Liverpool, but pressure from EMI, the
Beatles' record company, to release a single in the wake of the release
of the Beach Boys' *Pet Sounds* (1966) meant that the first two tracks
intended for *Sgt. Pepper* ("Penny Lane" and "Strawberry Fields Forever") were hurriedly released as what the recording industry referred
to as a "double A-side." As record company protocols of the time did
not allow the release of singles on new albums within six months of the

original release, this meant starting *Sgt. Pepper* again, with the first recorded track being "A Day in the Life," which became the final track on the album.[8]

Beatle biographies describe the gradual breakdown in the relationships among members of the band, particularly that of Lennon and McCartney. Faced with the problem of how to follow the success of *Sgt. Pepper*, the band started to work increasingly as individuals.[9] The result was a large collection of songs that, for Beatles enthusiasts, is relatively easy to link to their respective composers, with some songs played by an individual member either as a multi-instrumentalist or with session musicians.[10] Perhaps the most notable example of this incorporation of "outside" musicians was the inclusion of guitarist Eric Clapton on George Harrison's "While My Guitar Gently Weeps."[11] Once the album, eponymously titled *The Beatles* (but perhaps better known as *The White Album*), was ready for release in 1968, it became a double vinyl album. EMI were confident of its commercial viability given the Beatles' reputation, and, though not a conceptual album, it became the first of many albums that inspired future progressive rock bands who sought to break away from the format of the three- or four-minute single and of the long player being a collection of previous hits and their B-sides. The notion of a double album with a conceptual theme was later taken up by the Kinks, who released *The Kinks Are the Village Green Preservation Society* (1969), an album reflecting composer Ray Davies's nostalgia for the British village green and country lifestyle and criticism of the housing estates and office blocks that were part of the postwar expansion of London. This was not the Kinks' (or perhaps Davies's) first observation on British society; the Kinks had already recorded several successful singles prior to this album. As Kari Kallioniemi notes, Davies viewed the "swinging 1960s" with a sardonic, perhaps Orwellian, perspective that viewed the media-saturated race for postwar modernization as folly.[12] This issue was not lost on several later progressive rock bands; for example, King Crimson, Emerson, Lake and Palmer, Yes, and Pink Floyd (whose lyrics sometimes presented a predictive, and perhaps more accurate, view of Britain's future). Davies's songs that cuttingly lampooned the "swinging" 1960s scene included "Dedicated Follower of Fashion" (1965) and "Sunny Afternoon" (1965) (despite 1967's "Waterloo Sunset" presenting a softer, romanticized setting of the era). It was, however, the class statement inherent in "Dead End Street" (1966) that demonstrated Davies's view that all was not well in a supposedly classless Britain (in which lower class people lived on the fringe of new wealth and were often untouched by the benefits of the welfare state) that was yet to face the unemployment of the 1970s, when the financial boom of the 1960s came to a halt in the face of the OPEC (Organization of the Petroleum Exporting Countries) oil crisis.

ALL COMES CRASHING DOWN . . .

This crisis led Britain into a three-day workweek and the anger and frustration of the punk era that followed in the mid-1970s (see chapter 4). As Kallioniemi puts it, Davies presented a Britain drawn from kitchen sink drama, present in the 1950s and 1960s, which was "filmic, imaginary and anti-nostalgic" in terms of its past and present.[13] This was certainly not the case in "swinging London" in the post–*Sgt. Pepper* era,[14] nor was it the case for *The Kinks Are the Village Green Preservation Society*. It is worth noting that the Kinks later released the successful single "Come Dancing" (1983), which bemoaned the demise of the 1940s, 1950s, and 1960s dance hall culture, a weekly working-class social event that took place in local village and town halls in Britain, providing an opportunity for interaction between genders and age groups who preferred to listen to live dance bands playing covers of past and current hit songs. Kallioniemi's suggestion that Davies was anti-nostalgic is therefore questionable if one looks at Davies's prolific and varied compositional output.

In the year before *Village Green* was released (some copies are dated 1968, others 1969), the Small Faces, another successful pop band veering toward conceptuality, had released a single long-playing album, *Ogdens' Nut Gone Flake* (1968), a concept album named after a nineteenth-century tobacco distributor. Its ethereal content had no direct message but tells the story of Stanley (or "Happiness Stan"), who seeks to find the missing side of the moon. The story was narrated by Stanley Unwin, a British comedian who posed as a science professor on television programs and spoke in pseudo-scientific language. This album was also successful, remaining on the U.S. and U.K. charts for six weeks and reaching number one in the United Kingdom. Thus, thematic conceptuality becomes a frequent component in many progressive rock bands' repertoires, and it is worth exploring the background of some of the conceptual recordings that became successful at the time.

THEMATIC CONCEPTUALITY BEFORE THE OIL CRISIS

In terms of a double concept album containing a continuous theme, the Who released *Tommy* as a rock opera (the record company and media used the term "opera" to describe and promote it) in 1969, and this further set the trend for conceptuality in progressive rock. The Who had been a successful chart band since their first U.K. hit single in 1964 and had released three LPs, all of which were successful on the U.K. charts and, to an extent, in the United States. Pete Townshend, the band's guitarist and principal composer, already had composed extended songs. In the late 1960s, members were concerned that the band was largely regarded as a pop band by the media and the public, despite their reputation for destroying their musical equipment as part of what Townshend, who studied with Gustav Metzger at Ealing College of Art in London, called "auto-destructive art."[15] The band also had a reputation for a dynamic and energetic stage show and had been part of what has often been called "the British invasion," in which many rhythm and blues–based U.K. pop bands became successful in the United States (other examples include the Rolling Stones, the Animals, and the Yardbirds). Nevertheless, the Who were concerned that they needed a new public perception as an album-producing band in order to ensure continued commercial success.[16]

Townshend had composed "A Quick One while He's Away," an extended autobiographical fairy story in song form for the album *A Quick One* (1966), and he approached what the critics of the time called "rock opera" with advice from one of his managers, Kit Lambert (the son of British composer Constant Lambert [1905–1951]). Townshend is careful not to enlarge Lambert's role in the composition of *Tommy* and states that many critics and biographers tend to assume that Lambert had a large part in the concept because of his own love of opera. Townshend does, however, acknowledge that Lambert insisted on typing the album's lyrics in order to "protect the dramatic framework" as copyright for a future film of the music.[17] From a musical perspective, Townshend acknowledges that Lambert insisted that the album needed an overture that contained all of the central themes from the various parts of the "opera" and that it should be biographical and centered on a main character.[18] Lambert had plans to use a symphony orchestra, but Townshend was adamant that the album would only be played by members of the band. It is this point that makes *Tommy* confusing for the listener, because all the songs in the story are sung by band members. Thus, given that Townshend and lead vocalist Roger Daltrey sing most of the material, characters in the plotline are difficult to distinguish from each other, and the plotline is unclear.

It wasn't until Ken Russell's film version of *Tommy* (1975) that a story line became apparent. Although the Who's record company used the term "opera" to promote the recording in 1969 (it should also be noted here that the Who performed *Tommy* as a four-piece band at the Metropolitan Opera House in 1970, as well as at many major festivals in the same year), the work in its original form can be more accurately described as an oratorio, although *Tommy* certainly does not have a religious theme, except for when the lead character becomes a deity to his followers.[19] Also, although Tommy has an overture, several character parts were sung by a small group of people and there were no costumes or acting when the Who performed *Tommy* live. All of these components are integral to any opera and thus the description "oratorio" (or perhaps "song cycle") is more accurate.

Russell's film was critically well-received and featured several prominent actors and rock singers of the period. It also led to several theatrical productions of the work, the first in London in 1979. There have been several others since, although some U.S. versions have changed the plotline (rather than the returning war hero father being murdered by the mother's new husband, the war hero murders the new husband). The effect of witnessing such an event puts Tommy, the central character, into a deaf, dumb, and blind state in which no outside person could reach him, despite the number of disturbing experiences of drugs, pedophilia, and sadism he endures throughout the story. Whereas Townshend's original plot had Tommy emerging from his catatonic state as a contemporary guru, Townshend took advice from a critic friend, making Tommy a pinball champion who draws his followers toward drummer Keith Moon's idea of a pinball theme park, this time with more religious overtones introduced in Russell's film. It was from these suggestions that Townshend composed "Pinball Wizard," which became the hit single from the project.[20]

As what might be argued as one of the first major examples of lengthy conceptual rock recordings, the album was recorded in what would be considered basic conditions, given that studio technologies were making considerable advances at the time. Even though the Who were a major British band in 1969, the recordings at IBC Studios in London were always under financial constraints and Townshend was never happy with his guitar parts, as technological complications and time restrictions prevented him from completing them to his satisfaction.[21] Nevertheless, the album opened the possibilities of extended works to several other progressive rock bands, and it is significant that only one song from *Tommy* was released as a single, although the song has remained popular ever since.

ANOTHER RECORD LABEL ENCOURAGES MORE OPERATIC ROCK

Though technically a song cycle (a collection of songs by the same composer around a central theme) rather than an "opera," *Babbacombe Lee* (1971) by Fairport Convention was marketed by Island Records as the first "folk-rock opera." It tells the true story of John "Babbacombe" Lee (1864–c.1945), who was convicted of the murder of his employer in 1884, despite weak circumstantial evidence. Island Records promoted Fairport as a progressive rock band using the descriptor "folk-rock."[22] The band had established a reputation among progressive rock fans and younger factions of the folk audience for adapting traditional folk songs of the British Isles to a rock format. Despite criticism from the folk audience in general for adding electric instruments and a rhythm section to songs that were regarded as sacrosanct in traditional folk circles, the band has continued into the present, albeit with several changes in membership prior to 1996. This longevity is discussed in a later chapter.[23]

What makes the story of John Lee different from other murder ballads for which the band was famous is that the trapdoor of the gallows failed to open three times, and under British criminal law of the time, this was deemed divine providence. Lee was commuted to life imprisonment and finally released in 1907. Dave Swarbrick, Fairport Convention's violinist, found Lee's own papers concerning the case in a secondhand shop. Breaking away from their usual repertoire of reworked folk songs, along with some original songs, the band set Lee's experiences to music, adding sections about the helplessness Lee felt about his life, which was mostly spent in poverty. Although not as commercially successful as Fairport's previous and later albums, *Babbacombe Lee* and the story surrounding Lee inspired a play, a film, and a book.[24] Fairport Convention rerecorded the work in 2012, adding additional songs to the CD version. It is significant that the original single vinyl LP plays for forty-one minutes and twenty seconds, but CD technology increased the length of a recording, giving Fairport Convention the opportunity to provide more information about the case.

NEW TECHNOLOGIES AND INCREASED TRACK LENGTH

The growth of freedom of expression among progressive rock bands therefore expanded the success of conceptual rock music, which was becoming branded as "progressive rock" in the British music press. Although conceptuality and track length enabled these bands to avoid the pressure of producing regular single releases, this was not always the case for all progressive rock bands. For example, Yes released "Something's Coming" in 1969 and did not release another single until "Owner of a Lonely Heart" in 1983; Led Zeppelin never released a single in the United Kingdom; and King Crimson released "In the Court of the Crimson King" as a single in 1969, which reached number eighty in the *Billboard* Hot 100 chart (the song was divided into parts one and two as a double A-side). This was followed by "Cat Food" in 1970, the final single release by the band. Genesis released "Watcher in the Skies" as a single in 1971 and later released several major hits after the departure of Peter Gabriel when drummer Phil Collins took over as lead vocalist.[25] The band enjoyed several commercial hit singles. As previously stated, Jethro Tull achieved single success with "Living in the Past" in 1969. All of these bands, however, concentrated on lengthier works in a range of areas that would not necessarily be commercial in the mainstream. From the late 1960s, progressive rock's main progenitors were at the forefront of utilizing the technologies that became readily available during the 1970s, including new studio technologies, the distribution methods used for recorded work, and instrumentation and sound reinforcement. Moreover, without restrictions imposed by record companies on the production of singles, track length enabled further compositional experimentation.

Experimental conceptuality in progressive rock of the period is apparent on Genesis' fourth album, *Foxtrot* (1972). As previously stated, the original members of Genesis attended Charterhouse School and were an amalgamation of several preexisting bands there during the mid-1960s. Originally a pop band, they released two progressive albums (to a large extent influenced by Yes and King Crimson) before their membership was consolidated during the recording of the band's third album, *Nursery Cryme* (1971). Members by this time were Peter Gabriel (vocals, flute, and percussion), Steve Hackett (guitar), Mike Rutherford (guitar, bass, and cello), Tony Banks (keyboards), and Phil Collins (drums).[26] The fact that the core of the band attended a British public school (in fact, a private, upper-class school that was not government funded) implies that some members of Genesis came from wealthy backgrounds (the issue of class will be addressed in the next chapter). Significantly, education played a role in how progressive rock was both performed and received.

I saw Genesis five times during Peter Gabriel's tenure as vocalist. Unlike other bands, all members were seated onstage, which was typical for drummers and sometimes for keyboard players but not for guitarists and bassists. Thus, Gabriel was central to the band's stage presence. As the band became more established, Gabriel's stage attire became more elaborate, often involving costume changes that necessitated long instrumental passages, many of which became integral to songs and were featured on album recordings. Also, given the number of guitars used, including a twin-neck guitar played by Rutherford, Gabriel held audience attention with monologues that linked songs while Hackett and Rutherford tuned the instruments to be used in the next song. The content of these monologues often drew upon topics from history, literary classics, and Greek and Roman mythology, an aspect of Genesis' performance that demonstrated the level of education the band's songwriters had received.

Foxtrot has six tracks, four on side one and two on side two. Much of the lyrical content draws influences from poets and authors such as

John Keats (1795–1821) and Arthur C. Clarke (1917–2008). There are also biblical references. Using a Mellotron purchased from King Crimson, the opening chords of the album's opening track, "Watcher of the Skies" sets the progressive theme for the entire album, given that the combination of Mellotron, Hammond organ, and Minimoog had become sonic trademarks of the genre. The lyrics of "Watcher of the Skies" are based on an 1817 sonnet by Keats, "On First Looking into Chapman's Homer."[27]

Another song from side one is "Get 'Em Out by Friday," which can be described as a protest against the positioning of financial wealth before the well-being of the working class. The lyrics describe how financiers plan to reduce "humanoid height" to four feet, thus enabling more people to be housed in tower block apartments in Harlow, a town near London developed to provide housing for those whose houses had been bombed, and that was regarded as an unattractive living space by its inhabitants. The final line, which is not sung but is printed in the gatefold sleeve cover, is a memorandum from "Satin Peter" of "Rock Developments Limited" that advises financiers that they will be happy enough with the money they will earn on earth, though they should also invest in the church to ensure heaven. The biblical connection to Saint Peter is obvious (Gospel of St. Matthew, chapter 16, verse 18). "Watcher of the Skies" and "Get 'Em Out by Friday" are seven minutes, twenty-one seconds and eight minutes, thirty-five seconds respectively.

It is, however, the twenty-two-minute, fifty-seven second track, "Supper's Ready" on side two of *Foxtrot* that established Genesis' reputation for the composition of coherent, extended pieces. Although "Supper's Ready" is divided into seven sections, each flows seamlessly into the next, and the complexity of the musicianship can be said to rival that of King Crimson and Yes. Lyrics are thematically drawn from Greek myth (e.g., Narcissus changing to a flower) and the Bible (e.g., the apocalypse predicted in the Revelation of St. John [chapter 19, verse 17] and a reference to a "New Jerusalem" predicted in the Book of Ezekiel in the Old Testament [chapter 48, verses 30–35]). The music accompanying these lyrics contains several dynamic changes ranging from the entire band playing in a rock style to several quiet passages of piano and flute or piano and/or acoustic guitar and voice. There are also several sections of irregular meter (odd time signatures), wherein the band plays rhythms unfamiliar to most pop fans—another example of progressive rock's avoidance of standard "danceable" rhythms. "Supper's Ready" is not a piece of music in which any one section can be listened to out of context, and it demands that a listener hear it as a complete work.

Such was the progression of recording technology at the time that, despite the length of the track, another track precedes it on side two of the album ("Horizons" at one minute, thirty-nine seconds).

The total length of the album is fifty-one minutes and eight seconds, a longer LP recording than was standard at the time.

PROGRESSION IN TECHNOLOGY—HOW WAS IT DONE?

I asked Grammy award–winning mastering engineer David Glasser how a recording of this length would have been achieved on a vinyl album. Glasser worked closely with Sony on the early Super Audio CD releases and developed a surround mastering room in 2003. One of his awards stems from his work on a continuing series of Grateful Dead projects, starting with *The Grateful Dead* movie DVD release in 2004.[28] In his view, longer LP sides were possible, "but in order to cut a side that long, the cutting level needs to be lowered (potentially making the record noisier), and the bass needs to be reduced. [Modern] computer-driven lathes can nest the adjacent grooves very efficiently."[29]

It is significant, therefore, that there are many extended "lighter" passages on *Foxtrot*, which add to dynamic impact when the bass is played and also allow for more "time" on the recording. Several interviewees prefer the vinyl options that this process offers, as explained in later chapters.

Given the technological advances in recording machines that had been developed by Ampex in the United States and Scully in the United Kingdom during the 1950s and 1960s (first two-track, then three-track, and, later, four-track recorders, the first commercial eight-track machines appeared in the late 1960s).[30] In 1968, Ampex also introduced the first sixteen-track recorder, the MM1000. Many progressive rock bands in the U.K. recorded at Trident Studios in London, which had the first sixteen-track machine in the United Kingdom in 1969 (though *In the Court of The Crimson King* was recorded at Wessex Studios in London on an eight-track recorder).

The benefits of having more tracks available meant that most instruments could be assigned their own track and producers and engineers did not have to continually "bounce down." This was a technique in which two or three tracks were mixed together at an early stage in the recording process (preventing later changes) and "bounced" onto the single remaining track. This technique thus provided three more available tracks for further overdubs. However, the problem was that unless high-quality recording machines and tape were used, the technique increased tape noise and hiss. That said, *Sgt. Pepper* was recorded on two four-track Studer recorders. As progressive rock bands adopted technological advances in recording, audiences expected a progressive band's musical virtuosity to be performed in live settings. Advances in recording technologies, especially equalization, were also used in instrument amplification and public-address systems and were quickly embraced by musicians in the genre. While a sixteen-track recording afforded many more musical opportunities than the earlier four- and eight-track recording machines, new sound reproduction technologies also made it possible to reproduce a recording authentically in a live context.

Live recordings during the 1960s were not always successful, however, and quite often subject to problematic mixing issues in the studio. Problems ranged from underpowered stage amplification to public-address systems incapable of reinforcing sound in large venues (the Beatles' Shea Stadium concert in 1966 is an example, as is the Kinks' *Live at Kelvin Hall* [1967], an album recorded on a four-track machine that had to be comprehensively reworked in the studio after the live performance). The Beatles stopped performing live in 1966 after playing at a San Francisco baseball stadium in which only two thirds of the seats had been sold. The pressures of touring were taking a personal toll on all the band's members; moreover, they were aware that they could not be heard above their fans' screaming.[31] It is therefore significant that improvement in instrumental and sound reinforcement technologies in the late 1960s and early 1970s paralleled the growth in popularity of progressive rock on both sides of the Atlantic.

Two U.S. rock festivals, the Monterey Festival (1967) and the Woodstock Music and Arts Fair (1969), had soundtracks recorded for the commercial production of films for each festival, and by the 1970s the notion of an individual band being established enough to invest in sophisticated recording technologies as an ensemble had become possible as technology became comparatively cheaper. Some bands also purchased mobile recording studios, notably the Who and the Rolling Stones, whose own mobile unit became part of rock legend in the lyrics of Deep Purple's "Smoke on the Water." Other bands purchased premises in which to install their own recording environment. As well as their mobile studio, the Who set up Ramport Studios and developed quadraphonic sound mixing for live performance (sound from four sets of public-address speakers rather than just two, as in stereo) in south London in 1973, in which they recorded *Quadrophenia* in 1974. Pink Floyd established Britannia Row Studios in north London in 1975, although the studio is now located in southwest London. Emerson, Lake and Palmer purchased an old cinema in west London as a studio and rehearsal space called Manticore Studios.[32] Progressive pop band 10cc set up Strawberry Studios in Manchester in the early 1970s to enable the four members of the band to carry out independent and joint recording productions as a band (prior to becoming 10cc) and for other artists. Later in that decade, as the band became commercially successful in its own right, 10cc also set up Strawberry Studios South in Dorking, to the south of London, although by this time two members had left.

Advances in technology also enabled several seminal live albums, such as the Who's *Live at Leeds* (1970), *King Crimson—Live at Plymouth Guildhall* (1971), *Yessongs* (1973), *Genesis Live* (1973), and, in the early 1980s, Rush's live album, *Exit . . . Stage Left* (1981), which was recorded to higher technical specifications than the live recordings that preceded them. However, Pete Townshend regards *Live at Leeds* to be a problematic album. The Who had expected to use the Rolling Stones' mobile studio (the Who had not acquired their own at that point). Townshend describes the experience of having a technician from Pye Records arrive at Leeds University with a small, basic recording machine that did not record John Entwistle's bass on several tracks, nor some of the backing vocals. The same problems were present on an earlier live recording made at University of Hull. Townshend selected the heavier tracks recorded at Leeds University (whose refectory had better acoustic properties) on which the bass was present, and later both he and Entwistle overdubbed the backing vocals at Pye Studios in London. The album had many other technical problems, such as audible clicks and noises, but the essential live energy recorded by the band made the album extremely successful, despite containing only one track from *Tommy*, the rest of the set being rock and roll–based songs, some by other songwriters.[33]

THOSE WHO CAN AFFORD, CAN

With the availability of mobile recording technologies for bands established enough to afford them and the cost of hiring a studio with the latest advances in recording equipment being prohibitive to most other bands, it was success and wealth that enabled bands producing progressive, conceptual rock to weather the forthcoming cultural storm of the mid-1970s. This issue is discussed in the next chapter. In the 1970s, however, sophisticated technologies were not available, and there was an almost celebratory move toward a do-it-yourself approach in the punk genre. I primarily have used the term "progressive rock" throughout this book on the grounds that the music remains in a continual state of progression, experimentation, and evolution and because its performers, producers, and technicians have embraced the new technologies that have become available since the late 1960s. There was, however, a counterculture that evolved in the United States in the early 1970s and in the United Kingdom during the mid-1970s for which progressive rock was anathema and that favored a return to the do-it-yourself ethos of styles such as skiffle, which was popular on both sides of the Atlantic during the 1950s due to the fact that one needed limited musical skill to perform it. This was despite the fact that the U.K. and U.S. blues revivals and folk revivals—both styles requiring high levels of musicianship—enabled American skiffle, blues, and folk artists to perform in the United Kingdom as a result of the promotional efforts of British skiffle artist Lonnie Donegan, a talented multi-instrumentalist.[34]

Consequently, the next chapter discusses why a new culture that followed early progressive rock, "punk," was regarded by its followers as the opposite of what they deemed to be ostentatious, pretentious, and overindulgent rock music that had gotten out of touch with the visceral nature of rock and roll in its broadest terms. It also addresses issues relating to class, education, and social change in a period during which the expense of concert attendance, which was driven by the cost of touring, became problematic for audiences and bands. Moreover, it outlines why progressive rock survived, developed, and still exists, albeit often in a nostalgic format, unlike the punk of the 1970s, which was no longer viable after the Sex Pistols' 1996 "Filthy Lucre" reunion tour— an obvious financial venture during a Conservative meltdown prior to an election defeat. My own mid-1970s memories of a soon-to-be member of the Clash having coffee afternoons in my London apartment while listening to Joni Mitchell, Weather Report, and Steely Dan make me question the genre's honesty, given that musician's tirade against the music to which we had once listened in his first press interview after joining the Clash. At the time, I also lived next door to the Damned, who were quiet neighbors and rarely let their presence be known. In the 1990s, I was a member of a health club in west London, which was used by established rock musicians of the period, along with another member of the Clash who took advantage of the bar facilities but not the gymnasium. These aspects demonstrated the punk genre's frailty and falsity and its oblivious ignorance of the youth subculture from which it drew financial gain and a misguided following who believed in its power to make cultural change. Even during mid-1970s political turbulence, wealth was always a major issue with record companies, both large and small, and punk managers (and sometimes performers) often took advantage of the political downturn in opportunities for disenfranchised youth, except for Joe Strummer (rest in peace).

3

ENEMIES AT THE DOOR

Prog under Threat

PUNK IN BRIEF

Many late 1970s rock journalists (particularly those who wrote for the weekly music newspaper *New Musical Express*) viewed punk as the "antidote" to what they perceived as the technical excesses of progressive rock.[1] Still revered among its remaining audience and by the followers of the Seattle grunge movement of the early 1990s, punk freed the musician who desired to write and perform songs from the demands of becoming highly proficient at either skill, and it created a do-it-yourself (DIY) ethos among musicians of the period, much like skiffle and to a small extent rock and roll had done to the preexisting jazz styles in the 1950s. Though Hegarty and Halliwell note that King Crimson, Soft Machine, and Van Der Graaf Generator did not receive the same punk vitriol as Yes, Genesis, Jethro Tull, and Emerson, Lake and Palmer, they acknowledge that "prog is an incredibly varied genre based on fusions of styles, approaches and genres, and that it taps into broader cultural resonances that link to avant garde art, classical and folk music, performance and the moving image."[2]

While progressive rock audiences had come to expect all of the above, as well as virtuosity and spectacle, a new pub-based scene in both the United Kingdom and the United States enabled bands to perform in intimate venues and within a subculture largely encouraged in the United Kingdom by punk promoters and managers such as Malcolm McClaren, following his experiences in the United States managing the New York Dolls. What punks regarded as rock excess in stage spectacles was, for a youth in the United Kingdom during the 1970s, too expensive in a political climate that did not allow for the cost of concert tickets (the United Kingdom was on the edge of bankruptcy with high unemployment rates).[3] Punks regarded expensive concert tickets that funded costly recordings, stage sets, and expansive tours as being out of touch with their own culture. Thus, only well-established progressive rock bands survived the period. Though this chapter does not concern the history of the punk movement, it is worth briefly examining attitudes that some of those connected to the movement held regarding progressive rock that have become part of the postpunk discussions among cultural historians of the period.

Sean Albiez suggests a question of class specificity "of cultural capital and its relationship to the social distinctions of 1970s rock music—with 'prog' a cerebral middle class pursuit and punk a visceral working class revolt."[4] John Lydon (Johnny Rotten of the Sex Pistols), Keith Levene (the Clash and Public Image Limited), and the Damned, however, all had various personal investments in the music of Syd Barrett, Van Der Graaf Generator, Pink Floyd, and Hawkwind. In terms of being informed by literature, Lydon was also an avid reader and read the works of Oscar Wilde, Ted Hughes, James Joyce, and Muriel Spark.

Albiez defines punk identity as "at the cultural level . . . the outcome of musicians and consumers negotiating and commenting on the punk era through their own narration of commonly held, but differently experienced, stories."[5]

Punk exhibited the reality of underprivileged British youth who saw, as the Sex Pistols put it, "no future," and the music was accurately described as "dole queue rock." Unlike the Clash and their determination to emphasize radical politics, however, the Sex Pistols "never presented any coherent political front or songs."[6] Albiez maintains that "Lydon, and his later colleagues in Public Image Limited embraced musical changes in their music that are antithetical to punk."[7]

It is worth noting that progressive bands—for example, Caravan and its spinoff band, Hatfield and the North (which arguably preempted Return to Forever with its performance of "Your Majesty Is Like a Cream Donut [Calyx]")—were broadcast to ecstatic live audiences by the BBC as the band performed at the Paris Theatre in London. This concert took place in 1975, when punk was starting to emerge, and these recordings are still available on YouTube. That said, there may have been elements of parody and protest in John Lydon wearing a defaced Pink Floyd tee shirt at his Sex Pistols audition, although he later made an album, *Disturbing the Peace* (1985), with guitarist Steve Vai as part of his Public Image Limited band. Rick Fenn of 10cc recalled an incident with Lydon at a television studio prior to his tenure with 10cc.

> At the time that [my band] Gentlemen were recording our appearance on *So It Goes* [a British television program broadcast from Manchester where, coincidentally, 10cc had their own recording studio], prog was alive and well and, with the help of this TV show, we were confident that we would be soon joining the ranks of its elite. It so happened the other band appearing live on the show was the Sex Pistols. I believe it was their first TV [appearance]. To my sensibilities these postpubescents were unspeakably vile, and the noise they made was a total anathema to everything I stood for musically. So much so that I felt driven to tell them what I thought when I found them festering in the corner of the greenroom. Mr. Rotten parried with a tirade against us and it almost got physical. It remains a sobering fact that, within the blink of an eye, Gentlemen and their like disappeared from the face of the Earth and the Sex Pistols were as big as the Beatles.[8]

He added:

> I should [say] that punk had a point. Prog rock had reached such grand and pompous proportions that "the kids" just weren't represented by it or connected to it. The Who and Hendrix, in my day, came along and bludgeoned the establishment in a similar way, though I do feel that with punk, the lack of musical virtuosity was a pivotal weapon in its arsenal. And in the United Kingdom, the lack of technical prowess, with guitar in particular, became pretty much de rigueur for decades to come.
>
> But the best of punk or postpunk is great stuff, and like the best of any genre, it will survive the test of time.[9]

Many punks, however, later became associated with the "Oi" culture of the 1980s with its connections to racism and the British National Party. Original punk values and music still exist, however, and bands such as the Anti Nowhere League and the Damned continued to tour in the 2000s. However, if one were to visit Carnaby Street in the West End of London nowadays, one should expect to pay up to $20 to photograph a punk complete with Mohican hairstyle, Westwood tartan, and bondage clothing. The cottage industry of the previous hippie idyll thus still exists.

It is worth noting here that another popular style at the time was the African American–influenced "disco," which was produced on both sides of the Atlantic (and was often consumed by what Allan F. Moore has referred to as "the working class dancing market").[10] Although a great deal of this musical style relied on a solid four beats to the measure rhythmic structure with no change in tempo and simple chord structures, African American bands and artists such as Earth, Wind and Fire, Stevie Wonder, and Marvin Gaye produced erudite and cutting-edge recordings aimed at a more refined market.

IN THE WAKE OF PUNK

In the genre that followed, often referred to as "new wave," many progressive musicians downsized their bands and their stage acts and adapted to current stylistic demands made by an audience that wanted sophisticated pop music without the wrath of punk and that embraced sonic sophistication and memorable melodic content.[11] Despite the epithets used to describe punk—DIY rock, dole queue rock, and others—musicianship existed in some of the bands of the period inaccurately described and marketed as punk. For example, Norman Watt-Roy, bassist for the band the Greatest Show on Earth (which was signed to Harvest, an EMI progressive subsidiary, and which emulated U.S. bands such as Blood, Sweat and Tears and Chicago), joined Kilburn and the High Roads and played bass on the seminal pop fusion song, "Hit Me with Your Rhythm Stick" once the band had changed its name to Ian Dury and the Blockheads. This bass line owes a great deal to the Weather Report jazz bassist Jaco Pastorious's influence on Watt-Roy.

The Police were another such band initially described as punk, argu-ably due to the band members' peroxide blond, short, and spiky hair-styles, a punk descriptor. The band's music was, however, sophisticated pop mixed with reggae and rock influences. Drummer Stuart Copeland had been a member of Curved Air, a band whose members were gradu-ates of the Royal College of Music, including Darryl Way on electric violin and keyboard virtuoso Francis Monkman. Copeland was joined by guitarist Andy Summers, a veteran of Dantalion's Chariot. Other bands who had achieved moderate success also changed their names and, to an extent, styles. One example of stylistic metamorphosis is Stackridge, a band that had been signed to MCA Records and later Elton John's Rocket Record Company. Formed in 1969, the band per-formed on the progressive rock gig circuit playing a mix of what rock critics described as psychedelia and folk-rock, though without the same level of success of the folk-rock of Fairport Convention and Steeleye Span. Stackridge were championed by John Peel and also appeared on the BBC television program dedicated to progressive rock, *The Old Grey Whistle Test*, in the mid-1970s. Continual personnel changes, however, dogged the band's progress, despite the fact that the band produced five albums before their first split in 1977, a significant year in punk culture. The band reunited in 1996 and recorded and toured until 2015. One factor in the band's decision to perform again was that it had achieved cult status by the 1990s, as a progressive rock revival gradually occurred. Stackridge took on another identity, however, in 1979, with two of the band's original members forming the Korgis, and the band achieved moderate commercial success with singles on Rialto Records, Asylum Records, and Warner Brothers Records. It was their third sin-gle, the soft pop ballad "Everybody's Got to Learn Sometime" that established them in the new wave of pop music that had become popu-lar in the early 1980s alongside bands such as Spandau Ballet, Human League, Heaven 17, and the Trevor Horn–produced stable of bands including ABC, Frankie Goes to Hollywood, the Art of Noise, and most significantly the Buggles (a band discussed later in this chapter).

The Korgis (who were also later produced by Horn) split in the early 1980s, as the band underwent many personnel changes and several members embarked on solo careers (a common occurrence among many progressive rock performers following the punk era). The band, however, reunited in the 1990s and often toured with Stackridge, albeit with several new members in both bands.

In contrast, a relatively unknown progressive rock band active between 1970 and 1975 was the Welsh group, Good Habit. Although the band supported most of the major progressive rock bands of the period, they never achieved enough commercial viability to withstand the punk period, despite attracting critical acclaim and being broadcast regularly by John Peel. The band was particularly memorable because they performed in green monk's habits. However, two members of Good Habit, Gareth Mortimer and David Land, formed Racing Cars in the early 1970s, although the band did not achieve success until Good Habit had disbanded. The band had a chart success in 1977 with "They Shoot Horses Don't They" for Chrysalis Records. They released four albums and five singles between 1977 and 1980 but never repeated the success of their first single. Before reuniting from 2000 to 2010, several band members released solo albums and also became session musicians working for major rock bands in many styles (for example, the Beach Boys).

Nevertheless, as previously stated, only "mainstream" progressive rock bands remained commercially viable during the period. As Fenn puts it, "The true prog royalty were of course able to weather the storm—at least, to a great extent—and I suppose it is a testament to their musical substance that many of these bands . . . can, and do, sell more concert tickets now than they did in the 70s."[12]

A prime example is Pink Floyd, whose album *Dark Side of the Moon* (1973) was released on Harvest Records, a progressive subsidiary of EMI. EMI was a label that had had success with many 1960s pop bands such as the Beatles and that was consequently in a strong financial position to facilitate progressive experimentation. Its American partner was Capitol Records, which had also enjoyed the commercial success of pop bands from both the United States and the United Kingdom. Pink Floyd formed in the late 1960s in the heyday of psychedelia, and all of its previous albums and singles had been commercially successful. *Dark Side of the Moon* was Pink Floyd's eighth album and, in the authentic progressive rock style of the time, each of the previous albums had embraced the pace of development of new performance and recording technologies. By the time of the tour to promote the new album, the band needed three large trucks to transport their equipment that by now included a quadrophonic public-address system and what had become the largest transportable lighting system in use in progressive rock. The band had become famous for the use of technological advances (arguably rivalled only by Emerson, Lake and Palmer and Yes by 1973), but it is significant that the cover of Pink Floyd's fourth album, *Ummagumma* (1969), depicts all of their stage equipment lying on a lawn outside a country house. Though the equipment would be regarded as modest now, it was impressive for any band in 1969.

Dark Side of the Moon remained in the international charts from 1973 to 1988, making it arguably one of the most successful recordings of the twentieth century. There is a great deal of both scholarly and popular culture discussion about the making of the album that is beyond the scope of this work, but it is important to add that many of the album's contributors (producers, engineers, session musicians, and technical crew members) became famous in their own right for their contributions to the album's success. For example, Alan Parsons, who had also worked as an engineer on the Beatles' *Abbey Road* and *Let It Be*, became an established performing artist and composer in his own right in the late 1970s and early 1980s and is still touring at the time of this writing in 2017. *Dark Side of the Moon's* producer, Chris Thomas, also had worked with the Beatles and later with Elton John, INXS, and Roxy Music, among others.

What is most important for this chapter, however, is that *Dark Side of the Moon's* success provided Pink Floyd with financial security during what became a problematic time for progressive rock. Moreover, the album reintroduced the notion of hit singles from progressive rock bands into the plethora of pop music of the time (for example "Money," "Breathe," "Us and Them," and "The Great Gig in The Sky'") are still regularly broadcast). That said, the U.K. progressive band Family had several hit singles during the early 1970s, as well as successful albums, and there had been occasional earlier singles from other progressive bands already mentioned. The concept of commercial singles from progressive bands therefore existed but was not a record company prerequisite for commercial success. Pink Floyd continued to produce successful albums every two years, which in turn were performed on successful tours, and this continued into the 1980s. These albums include *Wish You Were Here* (1975), *Animals* (1977), and *The Wall* (1979). It was in the early 1980s, however, that divisions in the band regarding songwriting contributions emerged during the recording of *The Final Cut* (1983), which eventually resulted in Roger Waters, the band's bassist and one of their main composers, leaving the band in 1985 amid lawsuits that lasted into the 1990s over the ownership of the band's name.

PROGRESSIVE ROCK CHANGES ONCE AGAIN

One particular band that embraced both pop and progressive influences was 10cc. The band consisted of members of various successful pop bands of the 1960s, principally Wayne Fontana and the Mindbenders, which became the Mindbenders on Fontana's departure, and a group of multi-instrumentalists and singer-songwriters who originally called themselves Hotlegs, a band that formed in 1970. The band was based in Stockport, Manchester, and had a basic studio called Strawberry Studios, in which they wrote and produced songs for other artists. The band's bassist, Graham Gouldman, had already achieved chart success by writing hits for the Yardbirds, Herman's Hermits, and the Hollies. Indeed, all members had studio production experience that enabled them to work for artists as diverse as Neil Sedaka and the bubblegum band Ohio Express. The band also coproduced Sedaka's international hit "Solitaire" in 1972. As such, this songwriting and production team became well established as a U.K. equivalent of some of the Brill Building and Tamla Motown Records composition and production teams.

Upon renaming the band in 1972, 10cc, with their combination of skills, moved effortlessly between the doo-wop pop sensibilities of "Donna" (1973), almost lampooning the close vocal harmony styles of the 1950s while adding complex harmonies that would not have been popular during that period, and the progressive rock song "Feel the Benefit, Parts 1–3," which is eleven minutes and thirty seconds long and features all of the structural hallmarks of progressive rock discussed earlier. This song is on the band's album, *Deceptive Bends* (1977). It should be added here that two members of the band, Lol Crème and Kevin Godley, guitar and drums respectively, started working on the album before leaving in 1976 to continue working successfully as a duo. They then made many iconic music videos when this type of media became the staple by which pop and rock music was disseminated. For example, Godley and Crème made the "Girls on Film" video that established Duran Duran's career when it was broadcast on MTV.

It was at this point the band's new drummer Paul Burgess suggested Rick Fenn as a replacement for Crème. Burgess had been hired on a session basis for live work since 1973 and ultimately became a permanent member of the band. By 1977, 10cc were a well-established commercial rock band, but the sophistication of their material drew from several genres (including doo-wop, reggae, standard blues-orientated rock, and the intricacies of progressive rock) and stood out from much of the commercial pop of the 1970s, not only in terms of songwriting, but also for the richness of their vocal harmonies, which were a trademark of the band. As Burgess put it:

> In the case of "Deceptive Bends," Eric and Graham were under pressure to prove that they could make a successful album without Kevin and Lol, so the aim would have been to try and make an album that was a natural progression from the previous one. Their approach as songwriters would have been the same as before, but actual recording would have had the benefit of any technical advances. From my perspective, it was my first experience of working their way, which was to record drums first, along with the instrument that the song was written on as a guide—piano or guitar. I generally had free rein to improvise a drum part and play what came instinctively to me, therefore influencing what sort of bass line Graham might add later. My ideas would have drawn off my accumulated rhythmic vocabulary at that time, no doubt including any prog leanings I might have had. The musical sophistication would have developed as more ideas were tried out as we went along. The punk thing was yet to come, so [it] wasn't on anyone's mind at that time. [13]

This description echoes how the band had worked in previous years and was, to an extent, unusual for the time during which bands tended to record as a whole band, with overdubs added later. Two particular examples recorded prior to Fenn and Burgess joining 10cc are "I'm Not in Love" (1975) from the album *The Original Soundtrack* (which secured the band a new record deal at a point when their financial security was precarious) and "I'm Mandy, Fly Me" (1976) from the album *How Dare You!* Composed by Eric Stewart and Graham Gouldman, "I'm Not in Love" follows a musical tradition established by the Beatles eight years earlier, in which 10cc used the technologies of their studio almost as a musical instrument to create a multitracking technique rarely used on earlier singles during a period when technology was developing rapidly. The band recorded multitracked versions of three band members singing "aahh" sixteen times for each note of a twelve-note chromatic scale (if you sit at a piano and play twelve neighboring ascending notes, you have played a chromatic scale) onto twelve channels of their mixing desk. Once this multitracking had been completed, the band was able to produce a huge, choir-like effect for all of the notes they needed in the song. They also left the hiss that is created by tape multitracking on the vocal recordings, hence the "breathiness" that adds a human quality to the layered voices. Though quite sparse instrumentally (Fender Rhodes piano, acoustic guitar, bass guitar, and simple percussion), the density of the vocals made the recording stand out from other hits of the time, and it was successful worldwide. The lyrics might be described as a love song in denial, with guitarist Eric Stewart questioning his love for a partner while trying not to directly state that he is desperately in love with her. This is another level of sophistication in 10cc's songwriting techniques.

"I'm Mandy, Fly Me" is more complex in structure. In some ways, it is similar to Queen's "Bohemian Rhapsody" (1975), which begins with an introductory section that composer and vocalist Freddie Mercury based on eighteenth-century opera before changing to a rock riff-based middle section at a different tempo, then returning to a similar theme to that of the beginning. "I'm Mandy, Fly Me" is also composed in several distinct sections by 10cc members Eric Stewart, Graham Gouldman, and Kevin Godley. The inspiration for the song's lyrics came from a poster advertising air travel between the United States and the United Kingdom by a U.S. airline. They tell the story of the song's protagonist seeing the poster and being drawn in by the attractive concept it proposes. Advertisements for air travel in the 1970s, whether on television or in the cinema, promised a flight in which the traveller would experience luxurious treatment from subservient air staff. The introduction of the song is a spoof airline advertising jingle that is equalized to sound like a tinny radio broadcast (and is only on the album version of the song). Depictions of wide seats and restaurant quality food were common in airline advertising, as is apparent in a particular U.S. airline's advertising caption, "I'm Cindy, Fly Me," with its hint of sexual innuendo. The advertisement in the song, complete with the electronic bell sound that was often heard in airports to attract travellers' attention, was changed to "I'm Mandy, Fly Me," hence the reference in verse two to the familiarity of the jingle striking a chord (and the chord itself is sung with a rich vocal harmony). The protagonist, now travelling himself, has been "absorbed" by the poster and is now onboard an aircraft in which he is led to his seat, fed, and provided with all the services that air travel offered at the time. The traveller then describes a spinning world in which he has started to fall, suggesting that the aircraft is crashing. He describes Mandy walking on the water to save him from circling sharks and giving him the kiss of life "like the girl in Dr. No." He is then pulled from the wrecked aircraft, only to find that he had been dreaming and that he is lying in the street in front of the poster.

Musically, the different sections of the story are illustrated by the diverse changes in the accompaniment. Fenn, who has performed the song since joining the band, describes the complexity of the song as follows:

> "I'm Mandy, Fly Me" is a brilliant example of the sort of lawlessness that prevailed in the late 60s, early 70s—a time when a record company would support a band through several failed albums before dropping them, when there was no Stock, Aitkin, and Waterman [a trio of producers of formulaic pop from the 1980s] to tell you that a single had to be this BPM [beats per minute] and fit this structural formula. Artists were allowed to take chances and put out a single that wasn't just a copy of the previous hit. To build that number of tempo changes into a single took some balls. But then 10cc were not short of balls.[14]

It is the number of tempo changes, as well as several rhythmic changes, that makes the song stand out from other single releases of the time—and the song bears no resemblance to "I'm Not in Love," which preceded it. Following the radio-style jingle that introduces the song comes the first verse in a slow half-time (approximately half the tempo of the main body of the song) feel. Four measures of bass guitar and drums are followed by a melodic phrase that serves as a memorable hook (produced by a synthesizer and that sounds like whistling) throughout the song before an early key change into the first vocal lines. The chord progression under the opening vocals bears no relation to what has preceded them, another break from the familiar pop-record format. The electric guitar starting in measure five is accompanied by an organ treated with a "wah-wah" pedal, and the lead guitars in harmony play sustained notes (a progressive rock use of lead guitars that occurs throughout the song).[15] The question of whether the poster's onlooker would take the opportunity to travel by air is asked, in lush vocal harmonies, before the solo vocalist considers the proposition. All of this opening verse has the same simple drum feel, and the softly played guitars and bass are supported by a Fender Rhodes piano. The verse ends with the airport bell sound and the jingle, "I'm Mandy, Fly Me," again in vocal harmony, using the musical hook mentioned at the start of this section.

The second verse has the solo voice interspersed with the vocal harmonies and harmony guitars for the first five lines before changing to a rock eighth-note feel from guitars and keyboards and accented by a four-beat-to-the-bar measure on guitar, although the harmony lead phrases are still very apparent. This occurs during the section wherein the main character enters the aircraft and is fed and catered to in the airline fashion of the time. This longer verse continues to build in intensity before the lead vocalist agrees to fly and to be taken away. At this point, the intensity is replaced by the rich vocal harmonies with a softer instrumental feel that combines the main hook with a new melodic vocal line that describes the aircraft spinning out of control.

The middle instrumental section (this section is too long to be what is often called a "bridge" in a standard pop song) starts with multitracked guitar chords played as rhythm accents with the bass and drums before multitracked acoustic guitars (without bass, electric guitars, keys, and drums) play a four-bar introduction to the new section in clusters of three notes called "triplets." This section is played at approximately twice the speed of the previous verses. The acoustic guitar pattern is established over four measures before a piano and a bass guitar play a low note phrase for two measures, and this phrase is answered after every two measures by a further phrase played by electric guitars in a similar rhythm pattern to the acoustic guitars. After being repeated, the section moves to a lead guitar solo, again accompanied by the acoustic guitars for eight measures without bass or drums. The band stops abruptly in measure eight before repeating the earlier acoustic pattern with the low piano and bass answering the electric guitar rhythm pattern. There follows a freeform, blues-orientated lead guitar solo that ends after eight measures with a rich vocal harmony chord. The tempo has now returned to the earlier half-time tempo.

During the description of the lead vocalist's rescue, the keyboard plays an eighth-note chord pattern accompanied by a similar pattern on acoustic guitar, with a synthesizer playing high string-like chords. The same chord sequence moves to a two-beats-to-the-measure pattern accentuated by the bass and syncopated piano pattern (playing on opposite beats to the bass). As the lead vocalist denies that the whole episode was a dream, the band plays a six-measure sequence of two measures of three beats followed by one of four. The final verse returns to the structure of the second verse with harmony vocals in the final two lines advising that one should not be surprised to meet Mandy when flying and a repeat of the bell sound that precedes the words, "I'm Mandy, Fly Me." The song ends with a return to the acoustic guitar pattern and a gradual fade-out.

Although so many different components in a song's structure were unusual during a period that was about to take on a simplistic, "do-it-yourself" approach to songwriting and a deliberately basic approach to performance, "I'm Mandy, Fly Me" set a trend that at once appealed to many progressive rock fans, but also to record companies wary of the impending punk era. The contractual issues involving three record companies that signed the Sex Pistols between 1976 and 1977 are well-documented. The band 10cc, however, used compositional sophistication and made use of their performance abilities to endure throughout the decade. In doing so, the band was influential in inspiring many other bands in both the United Kingdom and the United States to return to complex pop sensibilities while continuing to use elements that were still apparent in progressive rock bands that continued performing in the 1980s.

MUSIC ON TELEVISION (MTV)—AND A NEW "YES"

When televised music videos became the standard promotional tool for new music during the 1980s, it was embraced as an innovation, despite the Monkees' Mike Nesmith's *Pop Clips* of the 1970s, two full-length films and two shorter ones by the Beatles, and weekly television shows by the Monkees during the 1960s, and despite several rock and roll films in the 1950s. It was radio broadcasting, however, that had been the mainstay of popular music dissemination for decades.

Ken Tucker discusses and criticizes album-oriented rock (AOR) of the 1970s and 1980s, maintaining that it was "anonymous" music suited to a "limited" radio audience and that it was "impersonal radio fodder."[16] Although this description might be applied to several bands during the late 1970s and the early 1980s, he inaccurately includes Journey, Rush, Kansas, Supertramp, and Gentle Giant as prime examples. It would seem, therefore, that he had not listened to Journey's high levels of musicianship and songwriting ability ("Don't Stop Believing" [1982], which holds the world record for downloads), Rush's combination of progressive rock and memorable hit singles ("YYZ" [1981] and "Spirit of the Radio" [1980] are two contrasting examples), Kansas' "Point of Know Return" (1977), with its Yes-influenced arrangement and keyboard parts, and Gentle Giant's lengthy list of recorded works that remain popular with progressive rock fans in the twenty-first century.[17]

Guitarist John Knightsbridge of the Yardbirds, Renaissance, and Illusion supports a view that progressive rock influenced many progressive pop bands stating that, "Lots of groups picked up ideas and themes from the earlier progressive groups—Rush, Journey, and Toto."[18]

This is a similar statement to that made by Deena Weinstein, when she discusses "the tyranny of music over concept," because metal videos contained a great deal of concert footage that, in the case of a progressive band such as Genesis, was crucial to commercial success, given the visual mature of their live performances.[19] The same could be said of progressive rock and many progressive bands that featured elaborate stage performances and took advantage of the new medium. Conversely, Ken Tucker states that the "absolute pillar of AOR" was Led Zeppelin, a band that could hardly be described as "impersonal radio fodder."[20]

FM radio broadcasting ("frequency modulation" broadcasting using VHF for higher audio quality, especially for music, than the standard AM [medium wave] radio) remains the industry standard nowadays.[21] Nonetheless, MTV (Music Television), which was launched in 1981, quickly became the new medium through which pop stars became successful, and it was no longer enough for a performer or band to produce a recording as the only means of promotion. Weinstein points out that MTV was largely responsible for the success of Bon Jovi, but videos were often more expensive than a recording (Alice Cooper's "Poison" video cost $190,000).[22] There were mixed views about MTV among my progressive rock interviewees. Bassist Nick Beggs was in a band called Kajagoogoo in the early 1980s that had a hit called "Too Shy," which reached number one in the United Kingdom and number five in the United States. I asked him his views on MTV, and he said, "I was a part of a generation who saw it as a new tool. So we embraced it. It had its good and bad points. But when they played your videos and helped you sell millions of records, I think it would be churlish not to be grateful."[23]

John Knightsbridge had a view that reflected his experience performing live in progressive rock bands during the 1970s: "I rarely watched then or now . . . don't have much to say on it except if the song isn't very good, no matter how clever the video is, I wouldn't be persuaded to buy the record!"[24]

When MTV was launched in the United States in 1981, however, the first video broadcast was Buggle's pop hit "Video Killed the Radio Star." This recording, composed by bassist Trevor Horn, keyboard player Geoff Downes, and guitarist Bruce Woolley and produced by Horn and Downes, had originally been released in the United Kingdom in 1979, and it featured several of the top session musicians of the period. As a recording, the single is technologically and harmonically complex. For example, voices were recorded through guitar amplifiers to suggest a radio broadcast. Downes used some of the most advanced synthesizers of the time, and there were melodic and harmonic structures in the composition that reflected the composers' musical educations (Horn and Woolley from their respective grammar schools and Downes's studies at Leeds College of Music), yet it was still regarded by the music media as a new wave novelty record. It did, however, become a popular hit worldwide.[25] The prophetic title predicted that radio broadcasting was limited in the pursuit of commercial success, hence Lol Crème and Kevin Godley's own success as music video makers, and the sentiment of the single was echoed in Queen's "Radio Gaga" (1984). Most significantly, however, the Buggles were managed by Brian Lane, who also managed Yes (and has continued to manage various Yes members, among other artists, to the present).

During the 1970s and 1980s, I was often hired as a bassist by an advertising company in London, for which Downes and Horn were part of what might be regarded as the company's "house band." I was hired to stand in for Horn because both Downes and Horn were working on what the other jingle performers referred to as "that single" (the house drummer is also on the recording). Once the song became a hit, however, I was made aware of the facts behind why I was hired and how Downes and Horn became members of Yes, despite their own ongoing successful recording careers in the Buggles.

A DRAMATIC MOVE

With both bands under the same management, it was probably inevitable that collaborations would occur. Downes and Horn, both fans of Yes, were unaware of the internal problems that were emerging as the band prepared to record a new album at the end of the 1970s. Jon Anderson and Rick Wakeman had composed much of the new material that, when presented to the other band members, was criticized for various musical reasons. The principal reason was that it was in a new, lighter direction and that it was not as rock oriented as the band's sonic identity had become. Anderson and Wakeman therefore decided to leave the band. Downes and Horn had been invited to provide a song for the new album and were invited to a Yes rehearsal at which Horn sang the new song while accompanying himself on guitar. The three remaining members of Yes were aware of similarities between Horn's voice and that of Anderson and entered into discussions with Brian Lane about the possibility of the duo joining the band. While Downes and Horn remained unaware of these discussions, which went as far as Ahmet Ertegun, the owner of the band's label, Atlantic Records, the remaining Yes members were eventually permitted to ask the duo to replace Anderson and Wakeman. The resulting album from the new lineup was *Drama* (1980), a much more rock-oriented album than the band's earlier recordings, but one that still retained Yes trademarks, such as odd meter bars, classical references, high-register harmony vocals, and Downes's use of new keyboard technologies, such as the Fairlight sampler, which was capable of recording any sound and converting it to the entire register of a keyboard. Downes also treated his own vocals with a Vocoder, a keyboard device that manipulates the pitch of the human voice. Howe's guitar work moved away from his clean, often jazz-like playing to a much more "metal" sound with a Gibson Les Paul, a Fender Telecaster, and a Fender Stratocaster (guitars used by many rock, metal, and blues bands at the time, although Howe returned to his signature jazz guitar, a Gibson ES175, later in the 1980s). This trend in progressive rock leaning toward metal is discussed in later chapters, but it is significant that Yes were at the forefront of the trend. The band became even more riff (repeated groups of notes) oriented on some tracks, with fast riffs played by Downes, Chris Squire, and Steve Howe either simultaneously or in answering responses to each other, with "Tempus Fugit" and "Into the Lens" being examples.

Another notable and critically acclaimed track from the album that demonstrates these performance traits is "Machine Messiah," a song credited to each member of the band. At ten minutes and sixteen seconds in length, it is another example of Yes' ability to create long compositions that continuously change in texture, rhythm, meter, and sonic qualities.

Lyrically, the song uses similar subject areas as those used earlier by King Crimson, Emerson, Lake and Palmer, and Genesis. Allusions are made to a futuristic, bleak, perhaps post-apocalyptic, industrialized landscape in which one realizes that winter is approaching because of the lack of sunlight reflected from buildings. The song refers to people gloomily facing an early start to a working day aware that they will be part of an industrial process—the "Machine." References to this machine occur throughout the song, echoing themes from Fritz Lang's film *Metropolis* (1927), in which there are two levels of existence, a world of wealth and luxury that is supported by a world of toil and strife, from which there is no escape for those who work in it until the worlds unite. The second verse of "Machine Messiah" describes how the power that lights the world also powers "the satanic mills," a reference from Blake's poem "Jerusalem" (1804). The phrase is used in the same context as in "Supper's Ready" by Genesis, although Yes' second verse ends by expressing doubt that humanity will "unlearn" their lessons. Although the following verse expresses a need for escape, the fourth verse ("verse" is perhaps a problematic term, since the length of each group of lyrics is different than each of the others) refers to "a higher Controller," arguably inferring that humanity will be controlled by a totalitarian

Big Brother figure, such as that suggested by George Orwell in his book *1984* (1949). The lyrics end with the suggestion that historical mistakes will be repeated as humanity waits and watches. The song ends with an air of acceptance; despite an opportunity for humanity to change ("Maybe we'll change . . . to finally unlearn our lesson"), the "Machine" will ultimately triumph and its "singular eye" (another reference from *1984*) will still be apparent.

From a musical perspective, "Machine Messiah" is, typically for Yes and most progressive rock, in several distinct sections. The opening section uses the dark, minor sounds of the Aeolian (natural minor) scale (play A on a keyboard followed by the seven ascending white notes above it, and you will hear the poignancy of the scale), with its foreboding and sinister inflections. Played slowly, the rhythm hints at a machine-like pulse until the section, which is in two halves, is punctuated by an Aeolian figure played at a faster tempo by the electric guitar as it descends through four octaves. This entire section is then repeated with the drums intensifying the rhythm with more fills and doubling the general groove that underpins the guitar, bass, and keyboard parts. At 1:04, the descending guitar passage, this time doubled by keyboards, leads to a series of syncopated accents (outside the constant pulse or "time" of the song's established rhythm) played by the bass and keyboards, while the guitar repeats the descending, four-octave Aeolian figure. Although the band's use of the melancholic sounds of the Aeolian scale is used for the guitar, bass, and keyboard figures that are played as an ensemble, the chordal movement of the central riff moves through the notes of the E Aeolian scale central to the whole first part of the song (E to F# to G followed by the same notes in reverse). As such, the scale is played simultaneously at differing speeds by separate instruments. Rhythmically, the entire section is in measures of twelve half beats and occasional groups of six half beats that suggest groups of three played over groups of four. This is achieved in a series of overlaying rhythmic patterns played by the band at various points.

At 1:14, the first major change in the arrangement of the song occurs. While the electric guitar plays a sustained melodic phrase, an acoustic guitar and string synthesizer play a three-chord sequence that is distinctly "major" (in contrast, "happier"). This new sequence is slightly simpler but much lighter in comparison to the preceding sequence, using a simple E-B-A-B chord sequence to support the first entry of the lyrics. These are sung in a high vocal register and in two-part harmony. This sequence is punctuated by fast tempo figures played by the bass and drums, although the section retains the same groups of twelve half beats interspersed with groups of six half beats, in keeping with the familiar progressive rock formula of polymeter in different instrumental parts. At 1:40, the bass and drums join the keyboards and the acoustic guitar, but at this point, the meter changes to six half beats in each measure, thus adding urgency and pace to the rhythm without changing the overall tempo.

Another change occurs at 1:53, when the entire rhythm section stops and a distorted, church-like Hammond organ plays sustained chords under the vocal pattern, which remains unchanged. By 2:09, the entire band changes to a shuffle pattern not unlike that used on the earlier Yes recording "I've Seen All Good People" from *The Yes Album* (1971) (at 3:32 of that song; even the tempo of the shuffle pattern of "Machine Messiah" is the same as the earlier recording).

As the intensity of the shuffle pattern increases, at 2:31 the electric guitar solos over the vocals. At this point, the shuffle section is interrupted by a series of measures that feature syncopated accents made of three beats played by the bass guitar and keyboards, while the drums continue to play four-beat measures in a shuffle rhythm. These "three-over four-beat" measures are interspersed with even more accents played by the entire band and are thus among the most rhythmically complex parts of the song.

This section continues until 3:00, when there is a lull in the intensity. The guitar repeats the long, sustained melody from 1:14 while the Hammond organ plays the main motif (melodic figure) from Charles-Marie Widor's *Toccata from the Fifth Organ Symphony in F, Op. 42 No.1* (1879). The vocalists sing the third verse in harmony, and in a form of what is often called antiphony ("call and response," in which one vocalist answers another). On returning to the shuffle rhythm at 3:30, there follows a synthesizer solo played over a four-beat measure followed by a five-beat measure (count "one, two, three, four" and "one, two, three, four, five" at high speed), with the fifth beat of the second measure played as a very fast sixteenth note triplet (a group of three notes). This grouping is repeated with the bass guitar and synthesizer exchanging extremely fast riffs built from the Aeolian scale and maintaining the same group of measures until they are joined by another guitar solo at 4:18. At 4:30, the guitar, keyboards, and bass guitar play an extended version of the preceding Aeolian riff, which is repeated three times under yet another guitar solo.

The dark riff that opened the song is played by a multitude of keyboard sounds, including choir samples at 5:00. The guitar now solos in a metal-oriented lower register before the acoustic guitar returns, this time playing minor (melancholy) chords over an open string drone, accompanied by a keyboard string-sounding chord sustained in a high register. The next vocal entry occurs at this point (5:54), and this is the section referring to a search for a "higher controller." Significantly, the intensity and slower speed of this section is in stark contrast to the almost metal style that has preceded it. The entire song seems to come to an end at around 6:40 before the electric guitar reintroduces the somber sounds of the main Aeolian riff that was played in the opening of the song.

Following more syncopated stabs played simultaneously in groups of three by all instruments, the band returns to the shuffle rhythm at 6:53, although this time the harmonic sonority is "major," suggesting a "happier" resolution to what has gone before.

There is a return to the E-B-A-B chord sequence, and at 7:06, the harmony vocals return. This time the suggestion of changing and "unlearning" what history has taught humanity may provide a solution. The chord sequence changes to a descending sequence dominated by the keyboards, and again the intensity of the instrumental performance builds. The following key change rises by a whole step, again reinforcing a sense of positivity. The rising chord sequence provides a vehicle for another guitar melody using a pitch shifting effect, contrasting the earlier lower register metal-style guitar solo.

The suggested lighter mood of the song is relatively short-lived, however, and the drums preempt triplet groups before the entire band plays an extended descending Aeolian riff using groups of triplets (more clusters of three notes) that culminates in a slow four-beat measure pattern dominated by the Hammond organ and with a return of the Aeolian riff played earlier in the song by the electric guitar. The Hammond organ chord at the end of this section is highlighted by its over-driven sound amplified by the rotating speakers of a Leslie cabinet. Minor chords played by the acoustic guitar accompany the Aeolian riff played by a synthesizer using an envelope filter (an effect that makes each note played start with a "wah" sound). Somber harmony vocals return at 9:09, still accompanied by acoustic guitar and synthesizer (this time played in a high register and with a string/choir sound).

The lyrics now refer to the aforementioned notion of accepting humanity's fate and are followed by the envelope filtered sound of a single note melody played by a synthesizer. The wish to see the "strength" of the "singular eye" is sustained in vocal harmony at 9:44. The culmination of all these sections occurs at 9:52, when the entire band plays a climactic and sustained E-minor chord, with the electric guitar playing the Aeolian riff from the beginning of the song. This climax slowly fades to silence to end the song.

Horn left Yes following the world tour that promoted *Drama*. He later pursued an extremely successful career as a record producer working with people such as Paul McCartney, Frankie Goes to Hollywood, Seal, ABC, Tom Jones, Tina Turner, and Simple Minds, among others. Downes remained with Yes and later joined Asia with John Wetton, Steve Howe, and Carl Palmer, achieving chart success with the single "Heat of the Moment" (1982).

A DRAMATIC END

By the next decade, in the aftermath of punk, both progressive rock and punk had undergone a process of change. Some punk bands traded on fans' need for a nostalgic view of the late 1970s and continued performing, such as the Sex Pistols, who reunited in the 1990s and again in the 2000s. As stated earlier, critics initially regarded punk as an antidote for the pomposity of progressive rock, and many lesser known progressive bands disbanded or reinvented themselves in the new wave era that began in the late 1970s and early 1980s. The most established progressive bands, however, remained active during the late 1970s; for example, Pink Floyd, Rush, and Jethro Tull. Jethro Tull often had major personnel changes, and the band moved toward more synthesis as Eddie Jobson joined the band, having left King Crimson, Roxy Music, and UK (a band that also features Wetton, Allan Holdworth, and, at various times, Bill Bruford and Terry Bozzio from Frank Zappa's band). Also, Genesis (with a changed lineup and a move toward a pop-oriented sound from 1978 onward) became more commercially successful with several charting singles. However, Emerson, Lake and Palmer disbanded temporarily in 1979, and Yes entered a period of hiatus following the departure of Horn and Downes in 1981.

More significantly, several bands from the late 1970s and early 1980s, which might be tagged in the criticized yet highly successful AOR and "radio friendly" descriptors, drew upon progressive rock influences to present a sophisticated and often complex alternative to the new wave sounds that had become established in the new decade. Examples of progressive "pop" sophistication can be heard in performances by Toto, a band made up of comparatively young but nevertheless veteran session musicians who had played for a variety of established artists from extremely diverse areas of music. The band still was commercially successful at the end of the 1980s and, despite various personnel changes, was still touring with Yes in 2015. An early song that demonstrates their combined abilities is "I'll Supply the Love" (1978), a deceptively simple pop rock track in measures of four beats until 2:45 minutes, when, after several ensemble riffs, the band starts a long series of fast-paced solos in measures of six beats, demonstrating the virtuosity of the two Toto keyboard players.

Further examples are Journey, a group of already established musicians, some of whom had performed with Santana, others with prominent jazz and fusion musicians, and still others with Frank Zappa and Jon Bon Jovi. The aforementioned song, "Don't Stop Believing" is also an example of high production values and progressive rock–influenced musicianship. Despite commercial success, Asia experienced continual changes in their lineup as members rejoined their previous bands, yet the band remained successful for more than a decade. Mr. Mister could also be included in this group of highly experienced, sophisticated pop single bands; their name was even a derivative of Weather Report's album, *Mr. Gone* (1978), and their lead singer, Richard Page, sang on later solo albums by Josef Zawinul (one of the founders of Weather Report) in the early 2000s, having refused the lead singer position in both Toto and Chicago.

Another highly successful band made up of former progressive rock musicians is Foreigner, a band whose individual members had already performed with Roxy Music, David Gilmour, King Crimson, Spooky Tooth, Keith Emerson, and Jon Anderson at various times. Although the band's first hit single, "Feels Like the First Time" (1977), starts with a familiar four beats to the measure with a relatively simple chord sequence, its long, half-tempo bridge section has a synthesizer playing a melody over a descending melodic bass line before returning to the verse. This verse is followed by a second bridge section in half tempo in which the guitarists play a melodic riff in harmony with each other (not unlike albums by Wishbone Ash in the early 1970s). Foreigner also maintained commercial success in "popular" terms for several years while maintaining their progressive influences.

To conclude, at the beginning of a new decade, it was "business as usual" for several established progressive rock bands. Band membership fluidity remained apparent, however, and although successful bands mostly maintained their sonic identities, others embraced a crossover sound that fused progressive rock with jazz, such as Brand X and Chick Corea's Return to Forever. Most significantly, by the end of the new decade, further changes emerged as progressive rock also became increasingly combined with metal.

4

A NEW DECADE AND A NEW PROGRESSIVE ROCK

The most successful progressive rock bands that were recording and performing during the late 1970s were still recording and performing in the late 1980s. For example, Pink Floyd released *A Momentary Lapse of Reason* in 1987 and Genesis (despite becoming more pop oriented and Mike Rutherford's success with Mike and the Mechanics) recorded *Invisible Touch*, the band's most successful album and highest attended tour between 1986 and 1987. Jethro Tull recorded *Crest of a Knave* (1987), won a Grammy award in 1988, and followed these achievements by the recording of *Rock Island* (1989). Other bands took a hiatus before re-forming, sometimes with a different membership during the decade. In Pink Floyd's case, despite the legal struggle over name ownership with bassist Roger Waters, the other three members recorded *A Momentary Lapse of Reason*, their first since 1983, using a range of British and American session musicians, as well as the three remaining members of the band. Although the album drew criticism as a de facto Gilmour solo album—the songs were mostly his and some had been written with songwriters outside of the band—it did achieve quadruple platinum sales, enabling the remaining members to continue to record and tour with a new and larger instrumental lineup.

In 1979, a band often labelled as postpunk, Marillion, formed modelling themselves on Genesis and Yes. They had a single success in the United Kingdom in 1985, "Kayleigh," which reached number two on the U.K. charts. Marillion established themselves throughout the 1980s as a new progressive band and, after personnel changes in 1987, have continued to record to the present day.

King Crimson was a band that had been in a period of hiatus between 1975 and 1980. Despite having several of the leading progressive rock musicians of the 1970s pass through their ranks, Robert Fripp had withdrawn from the music industry due his disillusionment with it. King Crimson had continued to record until 1975 and had enjoyed success with *Larks' Tongues in Aspic* (1973), *Starless and Bible Black* (1974), and *Red* (1975). Members of the band during these years included Bill Bruford, who left Yes to join the band, and John Wetton, another of the most renowned progressive rock bassists and vocalists (along with Chris Squire, Geddy Lee, Tony Levin, and Greg Lake). As stated earlier, Wetton left a relatively unknown Scottish band, Mogul Thrash, to join an established U.K. progressive rock band called Family, which he subsequently left to join King Crimson. He later worked with post-glam Roxy Music, Uriah Heep, UK, and Asia, as well as with Rick Wakeman, Brian Ferry, Steve Hackett, and Phil Manzanera, and others on individual projects. Other mid-1970s King Crimson musicians included violinist David Cross and multi-instrumentalist Eddie Jobson, whose career, like Wetton's, led him to perform with most of the notable progressive rock bands over several decades.

A "DISCIPLINED" KING CRIMSON REUNITES

After a seven-year break from King Crimson, Fripp formed a new band in 1981, again with Bruford on drums, guitarist and vocalist Adrian Belew (previously of Talking Heads), Frank Zappa, David Bowie, and bassist and Chapman stick player, Tony Levin, a studio veteran for many major performers, including for Pink Floyd on *A Momentary Lapse of Reason* (1987). The new band's name was Discipline, as was its first recording in 1981. Levin describes the band as follows:

> I was asked to rehearse with the group—I guess it was an audition—though I didn't think that at the time, in New York City. We all were very comfortable musically, so it moved on to writing and rehearsing in Dorset, England. First calling the band "Discipline," we changed that after a short tour to "King Crimson."

The *Discipline* album presented, of course, Robert's new direction of interweaving guitars. I decided immediately that the Chapman stick would be very useful in that, because I could sometimes join in on the top end of the stick, with the guitars, and on the bass side, its very percussive attack worked well with Bill Bruford's new drumming ideas. On the *Beat* album, we were trying to move away from having the same approach (whether we succeeded or not isn't up to me!) and as is typical with second albums, coming up with material wasn't as easy. Adrian, who had a lot of input into the *Discipline* material, had even more with the *Beat* pieces. My recollection of the instrumental "Requiem" was that we'd run out of compositions and felt we needed another piece to fill out the album, so we did an improv in the studio, which each guitarist then overdubbed to and titled it "Requiem."[1]

Improvisation gradually became more apparent in this King Crimson, given that the new band members' previous experience was unlike any earlier lineup. Whereas several of King Crimson's previous albums drew on classical influences that were infused with jazz and improvisation ("Moonchild" and "21st Century Schizoid Man" being examples from the band's first album), *Discipline*, *Beat* (1982), and *Three of a Perfect Pair* (1984) allowed the band a great deal of musical flexibility beyond where each song starts and finishes. Because some of the later live videos seem to have moved away from the original recordings, I asked Levin how much musical freedom was given to each performer at the time, which raised the issue of improvisation:

In my case, I've had a lot of freedom to come up with bass parts on most of the pieces. Those where there is a given bassline, composed by Robert or Adrian, of course, I'd play that line, although sometimes with variations. So a lot of music freedom on the bass end of things. When we perform, there is often room for things to change, and that's accepted as part of the King Crimson experience. It's not often that I go back to hear the originals of any pieces, but when I do, I realize that I've usually changed my part a lot.[2]

THE BEAT GENERATION'S INFLUENCE ON PROGRESSIVE ROCK

Of the three albums released by this King Crimson lineup, *Beat* (1982) stands out, given its title. Although the album's cover design features an eighth note, the album's lyrical content draws its influence from the works of several members of what is known as the "Beat poets" or "Beat Generation" of the 1950s and early 1960s.[3] The album's opening song, "Neal and Jack and Me" refers to Neal Cassady and Jack Kerouac and contains other references to Allen Ginsberg's work. The lyrical content loosely describes Kerouac's visit to France that produced his book *Satori in Paris* (1966). The word "satori" is Japanese for "awakening" and, for the Beat Generation, it implied the culmination of all experience. The book did not receive the critical acclaim as Kerouac's *On the Road* (1957) but it, and others by Beat authors and poets, is referenced throughout King Crimson's album. In the 1960s, Kerouac's work attracted criticism. Only in recent decades has his contribution to American literature been acknowledged. An example of 1960s criticism of Kerouac comes from Andrew Sarris of the *New York Times* who stated:

> If the latest spiritual adventures of Jack Kerouac lack the ebullience of earlier explorations, it may be because he is hunting down a pedigree rather than an identity. . . . Once upon a time it could be argued that the literary establishment was underestimating Kerouac's influence on a generation of vagrant visionaries, fellahin [*sic*] without fellowships. "Beat" was a movement and a mannerism, a dialect, and a dialectic. Beat preceded Pop and Camp as a burp against liberal rhetoric and official culture. . . . Still, the evolution of a beat bohemian style did coincide with the collapse of liberal optimism in the Eisenhower era, and Kerouac lent the Beats their speech rhythms to the point that even Tennessee Williams could imitate them in Lois Smith's jukebox soliloquy in "Orpheus Descending." Kerouac can still write a blued [*sic*] streak, but his skyrocketing prose no longer illuminates the landscape. He now travels alone, out of his time and place.[4]

Despite criticism of this kind, Kerouac's writing style had a profound effect on his fellow Beats, the counterculture that later became known as beatniks, and on the 1960s hippie culture, as well as on King Crimson's lyrics in 1982. Songs on *Beat*, such as "Neal and Jack and Me," "Neurotica," and "The Howler" (itself in response to Allen Ginsberg's poem, "Howl"), directly reference works from this era.[5] These songs use Kerouac's writing style, which is often called "spontaneous prose," meaning rapid lines of broken and often unrelated ideas. Kerouac wrote nine explanations about how to achieve this writing style, the first three of which are easily applied to King Crimson's songwriting style on *Beat*:

> Setup: The object is set before the mind, either in reality, as in sketching before a landscape, or teacup, or old face, or is set in the memory wherein it because the sketching from memory of a definite image-object.
> Procedure: Time being of the essence in the purity of speech, sketching language is undisturbed flow from the mind of personal secret idea-world, *blowing* (as per jazz musicians) on the subject of the image.
> Method: No periods separating sentence structures already arbitrarily riddled by false colons and timid, usually needless, commas—but the vigorous space dash separating rhetorical breathing (as jazz musician drawing breath between outblown phrases)—"measured pauses which are the essentials of our speech"—"divisions of *sounds* we hear"—"time and how to note it down." [These sections in quotation marks come from an experimental modernist poet of the twentieth century, William Carlos Williams, whose work, as well as that of Ezra Pound and Hilda Doolittle, influenced Beat poetry][6]

The seemingly rambling vocal delivery of "'Neal and Jack and Me" starts by establishing a date, 1952, and makes a reference to being mobile in an American car ("on the road" perhaps). The second verse (in French), describes "*les Souterrains*" (*The Subterraneans* [1953], another novel by Kerouac that came from Ginsberg's name for the group, which means "the underground."[7] Significantly, "underground" became another descriptor for early post-psychedelia progressive rock. There is a reference to a character called Cody—the name given to Cassady by Kerouac in the novel—before the song's French lyrics refer to *Satori à Paris*.

The verses that follow are all written in the "spontaneous prose" style, as are those of another song on the album, "Neurotica," named for a publication of the same name that promoted Beat poetry and was published nine times in the late 1940s and early 1950s in New York.[8]

Adrian Belew sings extremely fast clusters of seemingly unrelated topics that appear to be observations of a major city at its busiest, though with allusions that are alien to city life, such as wild animals mixing with taxicabs, perhaps allusions to the growing use of marijuana and LSD during the 1950s. Musically, this semi-spoken lyric, performed over a collage of free-form improvisation by the rest of the band (a possible exception being Fripp's guitar part) fits Kerouac's description of the "spontaneous prose" style. The only rehearsed sections are the instrumental links between verses. The bridge (middle section) changes the tempo to a slower pace and is a combination of four- and two-beat measures. This section is not improvised but moves into a final verse that, as with the first two verses, is almost free-form improvisation. There are two instrumental tracks on the album, "Sartori in Tangier" (not "Satori") and the final track, "Requiem," which, as Levin states, is completely improvised.

Given that much of the *Beat* album is improvised, subsequent albums with various members of this lineup follow similar modus operandi. After the third album of what might be termed the "Discipline" group, *Three of a Perfect Pair* (1984)—an album that, like *Beat*, received mixed critical reviews—the band again went into a period of hiatus. I asked Tony Levin about King Crimson's hiatuses and in particular about the change in musical style that is apparent on *Vrooom* (1995), *Thrak* (1996), and *Thrakattak* (1996) after the break between 1984 and the early 1990s. These 1990s albums seemingly contain even more improvisation. Levin explained the change as follows:

> The nineties incarnation, called "the double trio," had Robert's new idea of two guitarists, two drummers, and two touch guitars. Really a triple duo. In writing *Vrooom* and *Thrak*, we explored a lot of possibilities with that situation. Trey Gunn [the second Chapman stick player] and I worked hard to keep our bass parts from cluttering up the music, which involved a lot of planning on each piece and different approaches as to what each of us could play. *Thrakattak* was a collection of versions of the piece *Thrak*, which is entirely improvised aside from the front and closing. [9]

After the break between the mid-1980s and 1990s, King Crimson continued to expand their musical and lyrical boundaries, but further progressions in progressive rock among newer bands continued to emerge during the same period. In the wake of U.S. jazz-rock ensembles such as Return to Forever, the Mahavishnu Orchestra, and Weather Report (all of which featured members who had performed and recorded with Miles Davis), as well as U.K. bands such as Brand X (Phil Collins's band when not working with Genesis) and UK (with its combination of members from established British progressive bands), the combination of progressive rock influences that drew from the spontaneity of Miles Davis's experimentation with a variety of styles paved the way for more musical complexity. This was combined with improvisational freedom and even more sophisticated musicianship that further embraced a plethora of styles and an ongoing progression in the use of technologies available. Moreover, jazz-rock (often referred to as "fusion," though not the type of fusion that might be used as an umbrella term for styles combined in progressive rock) began a revival in popularity that has lasted to the present.

In terms of discussing further issues of improvisation, the British bands UK and Brand X produced a number of albums and were influential to the fusion of progressive rock and jazz (and even the combination of progressive rock and metal that started in the late 1980s). Brand X in particular were arguably one of the most successful progressive rock bands in the UK that combined elements of jazz and rock in an improvised format. Keyboard player and producer Robin Lumley explained Phil Collins's role in the band, in which there were often other well established drummers performing when Collins was unavailable because of his commitments to Genesis: "Phil was always a founder member; he did his best to appear on most of the albums and tour gigs, only sending a dep in when Genesis commitments unavoidably ruled the roost. He was a staunch member and never became fed up or disinterested throughout the whole thing."[10]

Lumley also explained how the band's first albums were composed—given the amount of improvisation—and how his role as performer and producer caused certain difficulties for him:

> On the first album, we put as composers all four of the band, regardless of who contributed most to a certain tune or other. But after that, and for all subsequent albums, we listed the names of the authors of tunes as they were individual musicians. Of course, there were lots and lots of improvised sequences during tunes, but we hung on to the original authors regardless, all equaled out in the

end. . . . [With regard to producing, Lumley handled it] with difficulty! But although I had to wear "two hats" simultaneously, it still was very hard being in the control room and out on the studio floor. . . . I found it a little hard to keep discipline. . . . I was part of the band with all the chumminess and at the same time had to wear the producer's hat to maintain the rule in the studio.[11]

Chick Corea formed the Elektric Band in 1986 and moved back to his earlier jazz roots to an extent. His choice of musicians, however, remained jazz-rock and rock based, with original guitarists Scott Henderson and Carlos Rios (Rios coming from David Bowie's band). These guitarists were eventually replaced by Frank Gambale. After a hiatus, the band reunited in 2004 and still tours. Perhaps the most influential of the jazz/fusion/rock bands that arguably can be categorized as progressive rock was Mahavishnu Orchestra. It was formed by guitarist John McLaughlin in 1971 following his tenure with Miles Davis, when he performed on *Bitches Brew* the year before. Davis assembled a group of musicians able to improvise spontaneously, which also included future members of Weather Report and Return to Forever. The album was critically lauded and various members were able to establish their own careers because of its reputation. McLaughlin assembled a five-piece band in which each member was an instrumental virtuoso. Originally, Tony Levin was offered the bass position but was unable to take it due to prior commitments. Members were Jan Hammer (keyboards), who eventually left to work with Jeff Beck; Rick Laird (bass); Billy Cobham (drums), who enjoyed a successful solo career after leaving the band; and unusually, an electric violinist, Jerry Goodman, who came from the U.S. progressive band Flock. Goodman was the first of several violinists employed by McLaughlin. The band's first two albums, *The Inner Mounting Flame* (1971) and *Birds of Fire* (1973) (perhaps borrowing its title from Igor Stravinsky's *The Firebird* [1910]), set the mold for the fusion of progressive rock and jazz throughout the 1970s and 1980s. The albums featured various styles ranging from the almost-metal "Dance of Maya" to the free-form "Birds of Fire" title track (many contemporary bands, such as Mars Volta, cite these albums as an influence). There were several lineups of the band as various members left to follow their personal careers, but as McLaughlin's interest in Indian music grew, it influenced successive albums. Also,

McLaughlin started using the newly invented Synclavier sampling computer keyboard, thus changing the band's sound.

McLaughlin's influence on progressive rock guitarists and other progressive musicians since the early 1970s has been immense. Composer and producer Steven Wilson provided an anecdote: "Robert Fripp told me once that he had to stop listening to the Mahavishnu Orchestra because he felt he was too influenced by them. And I think you can hear there is a point at which King Crimson and Mahavishnu Orchestra are so close and yet one has come completely from the jazz tradition and one has come completely from the pop tradition."[12]

It is significant that McLaughlin's experimentation with Indian music created even more musical fusions among the musical ensembles with which he has worked. Like many musicians during the second half of the twentieth century (for example, Josef Zawinul, Frank Zappa, George Harrison, Robert Plant and Jimmy Page, Keith Emerson, and Rick Wakeman, all of whom found new musical styles and new technologies outside their more familiar origins), McLaughlin is able to return to his original musical roots while consistently exploring new experimental areas, an issue that becomes ever more apparent in musical progression among other performers as well. Following the breakup of the second lineup of the Mahavishnu Orchestra in the mid-1970s, McLaughlin formed Shakti, a band made up from Indian musicians from both northern and southern India who were able to play music from the Hindustani and Carnatic music traditions. For McLaughlin, this area of musical interest continues to the present. During the band's existence, McLaughlin used a customized guitar with drone strings built by Abraham Wechter in order to have a similar sound to that produced by a sitar.

Despite the cultural upheaval of the mid- to late 1970s, as well as the inevitable ongoing commercial success of the more established progressive rock bands during the punk period, there were still many innovations that occurred from the experimentation of individual musicians and bands during the period, many of which came to fruition and were accepted by the progressive rock audience at the beginning of the next decade. Improvisation and even more combinations, or fusions, of musical styles occurred, and progressive rock maintained its progression.

The next chapter examines new technologies in the twenty-first century that enable a contemporary approach to sound reproduction (for both new material and for earlier remastered recordings). The chapter also discusses some of the newer progressive rock bands who draw upon past seminal works while creating a new progressive rock that is not always tied to the style's origins in the 1970s. Moreover, several of these bands have used elements taken from the complexities of progressive rock and combined them with metal styles providing a further identity.

5

NEW DIRECTIONS IN THE 1990S AND 2000S

Prior to examining new and already existing bands that were still active during the 1990s and that carried on in the twenty-first century, it is worth considering how recording technologies and audience expectation and reception had changed by this time. Album length, once a governing factor as to what material was included on a recording, was becoming an issue of the past with other commercial technological advances. Audience reception had also become a personal and private pursuit, as a new technology enabled an individual to listen to music with complete detachment from the surrounding environment. Thus, one's musical taste was essentially private.

Originally known as the "Soundabout," the Sony Walkman was first marketed in 1980. It played cassette tapes and enabled the user to listen to music in any situation, for example, while travelling, working, or at home. Music was recorded onto cassettes, which were first introduced by Philips in 1963 and that were available in varying time lengths.[1] A C120 (120 minutes of recording space) cassette had an hour of possible audio time available on each side, and thus allowed two albums to be recorded onto one cassette, albeit without the sonic quality of a vinyl LP due to the narrow width of the tape, an issue that eventually would cause the demise of the device as audience sonic expectations gradually increased. The initial major problem for record companies was that vinyl albums could be illegally duplicated onto cassettes, an issue that caused a severe downturn in vinyl album sales once the Walkman became popular in the early 1980s. This situation was partially rectified, however, by the introduction of the compact laser disc (CD) by Philips and Sony in 1982. Containing almost one hundred minutes of sound space, the first commercial compact disc contained a recording of Chopin waltzes on the Philips label (1982). The rerelease of previously released classical records was numerically significant with recordings from the 1950s being available as "new" CDs into the 1990s.[2] The first "popular" music CDs were released in 1982; they were *The Visitors* by Abba (Atlantic Records, originally a vinyl album recorded in 1981) and Billy Joel's *52nd Street* (CBS Records, also originally released on vinyl and recorded in 1978). For David Glasser, early CDs did not improve recordings noticeably:

> except for low noise and the ability to reproduce things not possible on an LP, like out-of-phase bass and extended high end. CDs [using] 44.1kHz, 16 bit were a compromise. Digital recording quality and capabilities have improved immensely. An example would be the Plangent Processes digital signal processing used on many Grateful Dead releases. It's a technique for removing wow and flutter from analog tape recordings. Truly remarkable.[3]

The progressive rock bands of the 1970s that were still commercially viable and still releasing recordings during the 1980s took advantage of CD technology and released new, longer albums, as well as rereleasing back catalogs of earlier vinyl albums on CD. Many rereleases came with what were often referred to as "bonus" tracks (songs not on the original album, remixes, outtakes, etc.). Ultimately, in the 2000s, 5.1 surround sound technology, which was normally used in cinemas, was introduced in music reproduction. This process is produced for the consumer on a DVD (digital video disc) normally used for sound and vision as a means of reproducing visuals and sound simultaneously. The "5.1" refers to the speaker configuration used to produce the remix image—left, center, right from the speakers in front of the listener and left and right usually at the rear, with one subwoofer (a speaker designed to produce only low frequencies) placed in a variety of locations for very low frequency reproduction (much like home theater systems).[4] Currently, listeners can enjoy up to 11.4 surround sound, although this is usually in the domain of cinemas and home cinema enthusiasts. Glasser is an acknowledged expert in this field and commented:

I am a huge fan of 5.1 sound. I've been set up to master 5.1 surround since 2003. When it's done well, it really puts you inside the musical space and is great for live concert recordings, which put you inside a concert hall or stadium. I've worked on some surround projects which really pushed the envelope and used the entire surround environment to place the musical elements. There are some excellent surround remixes of familiar albums—the surround mix of "Layla" is great! The coda has the dueling guitars of Clapton and Duane Allman in the rear channels while the prominent piano part is in the front.[5]

It is therefore significant that many contemporary progressive rock bands, such as Porcupine Tree, Dream Theater, Rush, and Opeth have all released, or rereleased, albums in 5.1 (or higher) surround sound. This new concept again exemplifies the use of advances in technology to keep progressive rock contemporary, no matter the exact definition that could be applied to it, just presenting it in a new sonic medium keeps it progressive. It is also significant that many established bands have asked Steven Wilson to carry out the 5.1 surround sound remix processes for them. These bands include Emerson, Lake and Palmer, Genesis, King Crimson, Jethro Tull, and Queen, among others. Wilson does, however, have different views on surround sound remixes than Glasser. Having carried out thirty to forty of these remixes, Wilson's view is that, despite advanced contemporary technology, the remix engineer must not take the process too far from the original, thus losing what the listener expects to hear, almost as a piece of nostalgia:

I've learned to do that by deconstructing and reconstructing these classic albums. And apart from the real extreme purists, I think most people are very happy with the sound of those mixes. Which are . . . kind of faithful to the old records. You ask how I do it: the first thing I do is I re-create the stereo by referring constantly back to the original mix and trying to match it as closely as possible. So if it's EQ, compression, reverberation, balance, any volume rise, the stereo positioning, all of that stuff, I try to be really, really careful. Unless I think it's just really wrong.

There's a couple of Jethro Tull albums I did where the original stereo mixes were those kind of late '60s stereo mixes where you have the whole band on one side and the vocalists on the other. So we kind of tried to make that a little bit more glued together. But generally speaking, I've been very faithful with everything and I've learned to re-create the sounds of the '60s and '70s and the '80s and the '90s.[6]

Wilson is in the process of attempting a simulated surround sound experience in live performances nowadays, but he explained the problems he has experienced in doing so:

> When I started doing 5.1, the obvious next step was to try and do that in the live context. It's slightly different because when you do true 5.1, you're mixing for someone in a relatively small space and you know the speakers are all gonna be equidistant, ideally. When you work in quad in a live context, you know that . . . almost everyone in the audience is going to be closer to one speaker than they are to the other three. So you can't be quite as experimental.[7]

Another musician/producer making remixes in surround sound of old and new recordings is King Crimson guitarist Jakko Jakszyk who, like Glasser and Wilson, constructed his own studio in order to carry out the remix surround process. He described it as follows:

> I've just finished mixing all this live stuff from a Jethro Tull gig in 1977 and, as we speak, I'm mixing the first two Bruford albums [Bill Bruford was the original drummer from Yes, and later from King Crimson, who formed his own band when King Crimson took an extended break]. I do them in stereo and surround. I did two Emerson, Lake and Palmer albums. I did *Trilogy* and *Brain Salad Surgery* and I've done some Crimson stuff obviously and some other Tull stuff. I did Ian Anderson's most recent solo record as well. I've built a proper designed place with floating floors and it's all been acoustically designed, etcetera, you know? So, it's a proper . . . and it's quite a decent sized building as well. It's kind of in the confines of [where we live]; we've got like a plot of just over half an acre so it's a building in that plot.[8]

MUSICAL PERFORMANCE SOPHISTICATION ALSO CONTINUES

Musicians such as George Harrison, Robert Plant, and Jimmy Page incorporated Asian and African influences into their music (classic examples are songs such as "Within You, Without You" from The Beatles' *Sgt. Pepper's Lonely Hearts Club Band* and "Kashmir" from Led Zeppelin's album *Physical Graffiti* [1975]). For Led Zeppelin, however, it was *Houses of the Holy* (1973) that defines the band as experimental and thus even progressive. As Richard Cole and Richard Trubo put it, "Firmly entrenched at the top of the rock music world, the band was expected by many fans to dig in and keep giving the public more of the same. But in *Houses of the Holy*, Led Zeppelin showed that they were willing to explore new ideas in their evolution as musicians, even if they were risky."[9]

Cole and Trubo go on to say that "In the 'Rain Song,' John Paul Jones . . . created a lush orchestration on his Mellotron that sounded as if it came from an entire symphony orchestra. 'No Quarter' showed their flare for the mysterious and the dramatic."[10]

The term "progressive" embraces both of these attributes—the mysterious and the dramatic—and the term has thus become irrevocably tied to the genre during the 1970s. This remains problematic, however. What is more significant is that the central ethos of progressive rock remained into the 1990s and onward as it continually changed as the music embraced new developments, both musical and technological. This development further raises the question of "progressive" as an era and "progressive" as a musical mind-set among its current proponents. Steven Wilson summed up the definition of progressive as follows when discussing improvisation in blues and jazz, blues being a genre particularly pertinent to Led Zeppelin:

> Well, improvisation in many ways is synonymous with jazz and blues, isn't it? So one of the two things is the root to that. But I think what's really interesting about that is important, which is that there are musicians that are curious, and there are musicians that are not. And the curious ones are the ones that they may make a particular kind of music but their curiosity extends way beyond that and it does feed into their music in ways that are not necessarily so obvious.[11]

Nevertheless, curiosity is one necessary approach to invention, and it follows what many progressive bands have attempted during the past four decades in terms of sound reproduction and further demonstrates the ongoing quest for new musical boundaries to break in progressive rock performance. Though musical curiosity may have been one of the earliest foundations of progressive rock, it still remains apparent among contemporary progressive musicians. Several bands nowadays classified by media as "postprogressive" formed between the late 1980s and the early 2000s and demonstrate the musical curiosity Wilson describes. Bands such as Dream Theater (a band that at one point covered King Crimson's *Larks' Tongues in Aspic*), Meshuggah, Porcupine Tree, Tesseract, Periphery, Cynic, Opeth, the Contortionist, and Between the Buried and Me have all experimented with various combinations of different musical styles (not always world music itself, but approaching experimentation with the same musical curiosity) in much the same way as their earlier "progressive" rock predecessors. Many of these bands, however, cite earlier progressive bands in their music, either by actually performing their music or by making references to them within their own music. A description follows of some of the bands' and performers' modus operandi, which provides basic illustrations of how what might be called "sophisticated curiosity and eclecticism" in contemporary progressive rock occurs.

U.S. band Between the Buried and Me, a band easily categorized in the progressive metal genre that has produced a series of recordings in that vein since 2000, has also performed covers by bands such as Queen, Pink Floyd, and King Crimson. An earlier U.S. band, Cynic, which was also progressive metal oriented but with jazz fusion overtones, cited the Mahavishnu Orchestra as a major influence during their existence. On close listening, many bands within Hegarty and Halliwell's "postprogressive" description, whether they are bands from the progressive period of the 1970s or bands that have formed more recently, acknowledge the tropes upon which the first 1970s progressive bands formed.[12] Some still use them in performance but, significantly, Hegarty and Halliwell support Wilson's earlier statement that the genre cannot remain tied to a particular decade, and they include King Crimson, Peter Hammill (Van der Graaf Generator), and Peter Gabriel, among established artists who have reinvented themselves.[13] As stated earlier, bands such as Yes, Rush, and Genesis have all, to an extent, reinvented themselves as progressive pop bands at many times since the 1980s. For Paul Stump, U.S. band Dream Theater successfully combined progressive rock and metal (calling the combination "progressive metal"), stating that the band was "heavier and harder" than other bands in the genre and that drummer Mike Portnoy's Berklee College of Music education became a "dazzling" mainstay of the band's performance attributes (Stump erroneously states that Portnoy was the band's guitarist).[14]

MESHUGGAH

There are also other bands that continue to experiment with all of the various elements so far discussed. Swedish band Meshuggah might easily be defined as "extreme metal," yet the musical complexities inherent in their rhythm section arrangements are apparent for the avid progressive metal listener. The band is sometimes identified by the onomatopoeic term "djent," a descriptor of the visceral chugging rhythms that come from the lower three strings of their eight-string guitars. The guitarists achieve this effect by using what is known as "palm muting," in which the side of the picking hand mutes the strings across the guitar bridge, preventing any note or chord sustaining and thus providing a staccato "chugging" effect. Although the band eschew the term "djent," the range of an eight-string guitar, with its standard high range and notes in the lower range that equal those of the bass guitar, does provide a much broader pitch spectrum. It was the band's use of eight-string guitars that inspired Tosin Abasi and Javier Reyes of Animals As Leaders to use these instruments themselves. The drum parts (played by Tomas Haake, who joined Meshuggah in 1990) use polymeters that cross what the rest of the band are playing. In other words, there are many Meshuggah tunes in which instrumental sections have the guitars and bass in the same meters but with various instruments crossing and relinking across different groups of measures. One example is the album *Catch Thirty Three* (2005), which the band considers to be a single song. This use of polymeter has the guitars remaining mostly in 4/4 meter, while the drums use superimposed irregular meters. This album has inspired several scientific scholarly analyses.[15]

In brief analysis, the band is perhaps only borderline progressive rock, with its main style being metal. Nevertheless, the tenuous link between what is accepted as "metal" by its audience and what is expected by the progressive rock audience remains a complex one. I suggest that whatever the definition any individual applies, the band's music is virtuosic and complex, and the term progressive metal is a better fit. Though Meshuggah vocals adopt the "death grunt" (in which the vocalist overdrives the voice in a low register) and the guitarists use the palm muting technique, both logically placing the band in the "death metal" or "extreme metal" genres, the complexities in the rhythm section suggest otherwise. In his discussion of *Catch Thirty Three*, Oriel Nieto explains the combination in the song "Autonomy Lost" as follows:

> the snare drum and the kick drum generate a superimposed meter by performing a complex rhythm that repeats every four bars. This hypermeter is followed both by the guitars and bass guitar from the very start. One could subdivide this complex part into four parts of 9/8, 9/8, 9/8, and 5/8 times, where the first three bars of 9/8 would have a structure of 3, 4, and 2 beats (total of 9 beats), and the last bar of 5/8 would have a structure of 3 and 2 beats. [16]

Although Nieto's description is deeply musicological, which is not the purpose of this study, for the informed progressive rock listener, this provides fascinating complexity if one deconstructs the density of the rhythms and places the tune and others like it into the progressive genre by virtue of its sophistication and virtuosity. There are other bands in this contemporary genre that have taken the tropes of metal into far more complex areas of musical form by adopting influences from other areas, including the progressive rock of the 1970s and 1980s. All adhere to the virtuosity and sophistication of early progressive rock while also presenting the new postprogressive audience with the aggression and energy that often define metal.

TESSERACT

Another example of rhythmic sophistication is the U.K. band Tesseract. The band is produced by guitarist Alec "Acle" Kahney and, like Meshuggah, the band performs music that has a link between what might be described as metal and progressive rock, and it would prompt a great deal of debate among groups of listeners if one were to pigeonhole them. Suffice to say, Tesseract use polymeters between what the drums and guitars play, although this combination is quite often reversed with simpler drum patterns and more complex guitar and bass parts. Also, the vocals rarely feature the death grunt technique, opting instead for higher range melodic singing and overlaying harmonies (with occasional references to rap). This is not the case, however, on "Cages," from one of the band's most complex albums, *Polaris* (2015). The song's lyrics refer to the breakup of a relationship, or a sense of being apart, with the singer acting out the regret he feels as the person in the relationship responsible for its demise or sense of loss, though also placing a degree of responsibility on the other party. Suggestions of no more sharing of secrets, no hope, and a sense of self-blame are apparent throughout the song ("I'm full of hate without a hope and vision"). Although these lyrics may be regarded as a familiar topic in any pop-related song, there is a great deal of lyrical sophistication that appears throughout. One line demonstrates use of English rarely found outside progressive rock when the other party, asking for a reaction to his/her feelings, receives the response, "Do you have the discretion, assiduity, freedom?" The main protagonist seems to have placed him- or herself in a place of rejection and now examines the consequences for both parties as they face their respective solitude and "cages." This reflection is sung with the death grunt technique at the end of the song.

Musically, the song starts with what seems to be a sustained keyboard playing an amorphous chord sequence, never remaining in a major or minor setting and often using suspensions (in which the third note of a chord is substituted by the fourth note that then returns [resolves] to the third). What is interesting here is that the album does not credit a keyboard player, although composer and producer Aidan O'Brien is credited for "additional composition," suggesting that he may have played keyboards. Despite the tonality of the keyboard-like sustain sounding similar to sounds of the Mellotron, it could also have been produced by a guitarist using volume "fade-ins" through a delay effect that produces keyboard-like sounds.

Rhythmically, the construction of the rhythm section parts provides an intricate and interwoven series of patterns between each of the instruments. A clean-sounding guitar riff enters at forty seconds playing figures slightly reminiscent of jazz fusion guitarist Pat Metheny's style or that of Pink Floyd's David Gilmour. That figure lasts until 1:21, when the guitar plays one bar of 11/8 and one bar 12/8, a two-measure figure that lasts throughout much of the song and is played over what the other instruments are playing. This two-measure phrase is played four times (eight measures) before the drums enter with the vocals. An electronic percussion figure in the same metric structure introduces the main drum pattern that initially uses the same two-measure figure, although the drums' main part from 1:55, when the bass enters, consists of measures of 16/8, 16/8, and 14/8. From a mathematical perspective, the emphases (in bold) played by the drums are as follows:

1 2 3 **4** 5 6 **7** 8 9 **10** 11 12 **13** 14 **15** 16 (or 4x3 + 4)
this section is repeated
1 2 3 **4** 5 6 **7** 8 **9** 10 **11** 12 **13** 14 (or 2x3 + 2x4)

The constant pulse of the bass drum best indicates the phrasing. Mathematically, this adds up to some forty-six eighth notes of the 11/8, 12/8, 11/8, and 12/8 in the guitar part but with intricate cross-phrasing between the two. The bass follows the same pattern as the drums, linking with the bass drum. From 3:13, while the drums play a steady 12/8 groove until the end of the song, a distorted guitar and bass riff takes over from the clean guitar part, playing a riff constructed from measures of 15/8, 15/8, 15/8, 15/8, and 12/8. This equals seventy-two eighth notes and corresponds with six 12/8 measures played by the drums. The total number of beats is thus the same—seventy-two eighth notes played by each instrument. This relationship continues until 4:47, at which point the drums continue in 12/8, and the guitar and bass play a distorted figure through twelve measures of 15/8, which equals 180 beats corresponding with fifteen bars of 12/8 drums, which also equals 180 beats.

Again, the connection between the influence of the complexity of earlier progressive rock is apparent here, especially in the use of poly-rhythmic figures. The use of the guitar textures indicates the contrasts used in the song as the intensity builds from a gentle beginning to a much heavier conclusion. This couples with the obvious influence from metal in places and even jazz in the introduction, providing what I have referred to as a fusion of styles, which is distinct from the much-used term "jazz fusion," and this is where the similarity to the curiosity and virtuosity of progressive rock in the twenty-first century remains apparent. The virtuosity, conceptuality, eclecticism, use of innovative technologies, musical sophistication, and musical curiosity are present in "Cages," all of which were hallmarks of early progressive rock. These elements are also very much apparent in the music of many "postprogressive" bands, some of which have performed since the late 1980s.

Again using the mathematical concept inherent in much music and in a similar vein to Tesseract, Jakko Jakszyk states that King Crimson often follows a similar system of equations in their music, "[it is] unbelievably scary, not least of which because I'm playing alternate bars of ten and eleven whilst everybody else is playing in seven. When we first started rehearsing it, I had no idea whether I'd played it correctly until about bar one-hundred-and-something, where we all supposedly land on the same downbeat."[17]

This may be a reason that progressive rock, in all its forms, is attractive to musicians and audiences seeking challenging rock music. It is challenging and requires the approach of the musical virtuoso. The term "progressive," however, is not always regarded as relevant by some performers whose audiences regard them as such.

STEVEN WILSON

This is true of Steven Wilson's opinion of his music, which, while more stylistically and dynamically varied than the aforementioned bands, contains a number of elements that might label it as "traditionally progressive." That is to say, it contains tropes from a number of musical elements from the 1970s, but it also has a number of more contemporary areas that might be regarded as modern "soundscapes." Wilson uses a reasonably standard instrumentation both on recordings and in live performance. Some of his songs are reminiscent of his early progressive influences, others are almost pop songs, and still others draw on the jazz fusion of Chick Corea and Josef Zawinul. It is worth noting here that Adam Holzman, Wilson's keyboard player, worked with Miles Davis for four years and eventually became his musical director. Holzman has also performed with Chaka Khan, Marcus Miller, and Lenny White, among others.[18] It is therefore inevitable that Holzman's jazz and

African American rhythm and blues backgrounds should make themselves apparent in Wilson's music.[19] Of all the interviewees, Wilson was probably the most eclectic in his musical tastes, which range from Prince to David Bowie to Frank Zappa. In fact, Zappa's former drummer Chad Wackerman performs on one track of *Hand.Cannot.Erase* (2015).

Wilson is outspoken about how his music is defined but it is enough to explore at this point some of the diversity that appears in his compositions. He said that he finds it difficult to compose with others, so he produces demo recordings of his songs that he then gives to his musicians to learn. Suggested listening includes "Luminol" from *The Raven That Refused to Sing* (2013) that, at twelve minutes and ten seconds, combines a complex rhythm section with a coarse punk-sounding bass line. This is superimposed by a legato, jazz-infused flute part that is followed by a keyboard solo played on a Fender Rhodes piano, all interspersed with fills from an analog synthesizer (both remnants of the 1970s). A powerful rock guitar–led chord progression is followed by a riff that is eventually played in unison by the entire band before a 3/4 meter section played by electric guitars in harmony lowers the song dynamically to a passage with the two electric guitars (one soloing, one playing the chord sequence) under a lead vocal part that is accompanied by close vocal harmonies. This section continues with a flute solo playing another jazz-oriented style. The slow, softer section then continues with an acoustic piano solo followed by a rich harmony vocal section almost reminiscent of the Beach Boys. The Mellotron is then introduced very prominently over measures of 3/4 and 5/4. While this metric combination would seem like 4/4 in the Mellotron part, the phrasing of the rhythm section indicates otherwise. An electric guitar adds to the almost orchestral drama. Again, the dynamism breaks down to a piano interlude before a return to the unison riff played earlier. The song ends with exchanges between a guitar solo and the unison riff played by the whole band and then a return to the softer, 3/4 section that closes the song.

With a song that lasts more than twelve minutes and with such a complex arrangement, one might argue that it contains all the descriptors of earlier progressive rock. However, Wilson puts it this way:

I think a lot of people now think of that as one of the hallmarks of what we call progressive rock. Your piece of music might be ten minutes long, it might take up a whole side of an album, it has this sense . . . which I guess very much comes from the classical music form of journey to it and of storytelling to it. So that it is analogous to someone sitting down and writing a novel or someone making a feature-length movie. And I think that's a beautiful thing about music that you can do that, and it seems a shame in a way to me that it's not more embraced by modern music makers. I guess part of that is because the attention spans get shorter and shorter and it's harder and harder to sell music that doesn't capture you in thirty seconds. I can go to pretty much any country in the world and play to at least a reasonable audience, and this tells me there is still an appetite for that music that, as I say, is analogous to moviemaking and writing novels.[20]

From this statement, it seems that Wilson simply sees stylistic boundaries imposed by others as confining and that his music takes him where it wants to go without him having to conform to what the audience, the media, or the music industry expects. With regard to the jazz fusion influences on certain tracks, they are apparent on "Remainder the Black Dog" from *Grace for Drowning* (2011), with its almost continual atonal piano figure gradually feeding into the band's accompaniment with a prominent Fender Rhodes piano again reminiscent of 1970s jazz fusion. There is a free-form jazz solo soprano saxophone at 3:44, again joined by a fast, atonal riff from the rest of the band as the solo progresses. Steve Hackett's drummer Gary O'Toole maintains that jazz is often an influence on contemporary progressive rock, particularly in Wilson's compositions. He suggests that "if you take Steven Wilson as the example, I feel his jazz sensibilities have been in evidence since Porcupine Tree. I believe the [musical] world is travelling full circle in many respects, probably due to the limitations of the progressions of rock, although I feel the need to express beyond what earlier bands have done is a logical extension."[21]

On the other hand, Wilson's later influences are apparent on the instrumental "Vermillioncore" on *4½* (2016), a mix of fast riffing from the entire band that fuses 1970s roots with what might be seen as contemporary progressive metal. Wilson sees the direction of such tracks as follows:

Grace for Drowning . . . it's an album where I was really tapping in, for the first time in my career really, to my love of . . . the first five years of what we call "jazz rock." And I really believe that there was this golden era of jazz rock, '69 to '74, '75. And after that, I'm afraid jazz rock completely lost me. But that period is just amazing. It has this kind of luminescent quality. Partly because of using things like Fender Rhodes. Partly because of using things like Space Echoes [a Roland echo effect unit] and things. You need to watch what Chick Corea was doing with Miles, for example, on those early '70s records. And people like Zawinul. Fender Rhodes had this beautiful kind of crystallized quality, and I started to use that on *Grace for Drowning*.[22]

One of Wilson's most recent recordings, *Hand.Cannot.Erase*, uses a true story as a basis for his lyrical construction of each song on the album. It concerns a young woman who was popular but living in a city where she became isolated. She disappeared from her circle of friends and no one noticed. Her dead body was found in her flat three years later. Wilson's lyrics are sung from the perspective of a friend, as if the friend is looking at the dead person and their relationship in retrospect. Some of the vocals are sung by Ninet Tayeb, one of Wilson's most recent collaborators. In a similar modus operandi to his previous band, Porcupine Tree, Wilson remains a prolific songwriter and a multi-instrumentalist who undertakes lengthy periods of touring. The *Hand.Cannot.Erase* tour lasted almost two years.[23] As with some of the bands already mentioned, Wilson is able to surround himself with instrumentalists who have established their own reputations prior to working with him. For example, other than Holzman and drummer Marco Minnemann of Joe Satriani's band, Wilson has Nick Beggs of Steve Hackett's band playing bass guitar, guitar, and Chapman stick and, since 2015, David Kilminster on guitar, who spent eight years as Roger Water's guitar player. Kilminster replaced Guthrie Govan, who has become a part of the G4 concerts (at the time of writing) with Steve Vai and Joe Satriani.

ANIMALS AS LEADERS

In terms of embracing new technology, instrumental innovation, and combining a fusion of styles seamlessly, U.S. instrumental trio Animals As Leaders are hard to define but certainly have the tropes of progressive rock, progressive metal, jazz, and even neoclassical styles in their music. Two tracks from albums nine years apart demonstrate the diversity of sophistication in the band members' musicality as well as their versatility. The band has close ties to the progressive metal band Periphery, and various members of that band have programmed drum parts or played bass for Animals As Leaders. Most often, however, nowadays the band does not use a bassist and relies on the low sonic range of their twin eight-string guitars.

The band's first eponymously titled album (2009) mainly featured guitarist Tosin Abasi, a graduate of the Atlanta School of Music, who played most of the guitar and bass parts while Misha Mansoor of Periphery programmed the drum arrangements, added some synthesizer textures, and coproduced the album. Subsequent albums have featured a second guitarist (also on eight-string guitar), Javier Reyes. The current drummer is Matt Garstka, a graduate of Berklee College of Music. Given that both Abasi and Garstka have experienced formal music educations, it is not surprising that the band's music moves effortlessly through a number of styles, a trait common in progressive and postprogressive rock.

Animals As Leaders' first album gives an indication of what would follow on later albums with diversity and eclecticism featured throughout. An example that demonstrates this diversity is "On Impulse," a piece that opens with a clean-sounding guitar playing a picked melody in the middle to high register before an electronic drum loop enters at 1:24. The main drum pattern enters at 1:36 with the other guitars and bass. Dynamically, the tune has several contours but the central clean-sounding melody remains until 3:30, when there is a jazz fusion–influenced solo that takes over from every guitar part that has preceded it. At 3:50, the same guitar returns to a unimprovised arrangement and plays a melodic part reminiscent of the opening clean melody, although the number of notes played is less, given the complexity of all the percussion parts being played. This almost metal section then incorporates the clean introduction melody as a kind of recapitulation (going back to figures played earlier in the piece). This section is followed by a unison riff by all instruments before the electric guitar melody returns for the fade-out.

The band's pieces are usually between four to six minutes long; a contrast is the track "Modern Meat," a piece played on a classical nylon-strung guitar that combines the textures of classical guitar performance but with jazz influences. Unlike many progressive rock pieces, it is slightly more than two minutes long.

As of 2017, the band has released four albums. *Animals As Leaders* was followed by *Weightless* in 2011. By this time, the band's membership included Reyes and drummer Navene Koperweis, who was replaced by Garstka. *The Joy of Motion* was released in 2014. On the tracks "Air Chrysalis," "Physical Education," "Crescent," and "The Woven Web," one of the guitarists uses what has become known since the 1950s and 1960s as the "slap" technique. This is most often a bass style that has its roots among the rockabilly double bassists of the 1950s, who in an effort to be heard above amplified guitars and loud drum kits, pulled each string away from the fingerboard and let it "slap" back, which created a percussive bassline. Another method was to slap the palm of the hand onto all four double bass strings, again creating a percussive rhythm on the bass. This style was taken up by Sly Stone bass guitarist Larry Graham (among others) in the late 1960s, and it became a mainstay of 1970s jazz funk fusion, with bassists such as Stanley Clarke (Chick Corea) and Paul Jackson (Herbie Hancock) among the leaders using the technique.

It is unusual for guitarists to use this style but Animals As Leaders use the technique with a combination of slapping the lowest strings and pulling the lowest strings away from the fingerboard and releasing them, both with the thumb and forefinger of the picking hand. The use of this technique further enables the band to give the impression of the presence of a bassist.

The band's latest album, *The Madness of Many* (2016) features a piece called "The Brain Dance" that, like "Modern Meat," predominantly features a nylon-strung guitar that remains at the forefront of the track even with a complex drum part (mostly 6/8 meter based) and an electric guitar that enters at 1:56 and is riff based in a progressive metal style. The nylon-strung guitar plays a looped figure (fast repetitions of the same figure that may be played by a band member but could also be achieved with a looping effect unit) before returning to a melodic figure similar to that at the beginning of the track. Again, the track is comparatively short (at 3:51) despite its complexity and the number of guitar parts that link together to create an interwoven piece of counterpoint (complex but complementary harmonies from both guitars).

In conclusion, the bands discussed in this chapter are a few of the most successful postprogressive bands currently recording and performing live. Although close scrutiny of some of their albums might point to influences from earlier progressive bands, the issue of whether these progressive rock influences are acknowledged or not is less important than the continuum of musical experimentation and combinations of styles in areas avoided by the pop mainstream. The material produced by these bands is due to musical knowledge in most cases, but in all cases it is a result of musical curiosity, a trait that has been apparent in the genre since its emergence in the late 1960s.

Although this book so far mainly has focused on the experience of listening to progressive rock, the next chapter addresses the visual experience that developed in tandem with performance technologies during the early days of the genre, and how one particular European band that is arguably on the cusp of postprogressive rock has used cinematic and historical approaches to highlight live performances.

6

TRIPPING THE LIGHT FANTASTIC

Progressive Rock and Spectacle

During the late 1960s, the psychedelic period in the United States and the United Kingdom featured visual art as much it did music. Posters advertising performances, clothing, album cover art, and much of the associated ephemera surrounding the period concerned the re-creation of the "acid" experience, or the notion of what it might be like. Pink Floyd's first album cover for *Piper at the Gates of Dawn* (1967) attempted to do this with a collage of split images of the band. At psychedelic concerts, the light show became an integral part of any rock show, often referred to as "happenings." As discussed earlier, Joe's Lights were influential in the psychedelic period that preceded the progressive rock era and had an effect on how it was presented in live performance. Pink Floyd were among the late 1960s bands that would improvise at all-night concerts in venues that had no "follow spots" (spotlights that feature individual musicians); instead bands were bathed in multicolored lights that continually changed as the glass lenses containing the colored oils rotated in front of the projectors. Again, as previously stated, Dantalion's Chariot was a band aware of the visual experience at a live performance being as important as the auditory one. The band dressed in white stage attire to highlight the projected colors, as did Principal Edward's Magic Theatre, a band that lived as a commune and were supported by the DJ John Peel, who signed them to his label, Dandelion Records. Principal Edward's Magic Theatre presented the audience not only with a progressive rock performance, but also a theatrical production.

The trend in visual presentation accompanying a musical performance transferred easily to progressive rock, and the first incarnation of King Crimson had a lighting engineer who was also the band's lyricist. Peter Sinfield was credited as the creator of "words and illumination" on album sleeves to acknowledge his contribution to both. Also, Crimson's first album, *In the Court of the Crimson King* (1969) had a cover highly influenced by the lighting techniques used by the band that has since become seminal to the band's identity.

GENESIS LIVE

Though Genesis had several instrument changes and tunings that took place between songs during live performances, vocalist Peter Gabriel gave a series of monologues that he used to link songs or introduce songs. As the band became more commercially successful, however, Gabriel started to include elaborate costume changes, often relating to characters in the band's songs. Most of the band remained seated and wore white clothing, but Gabriel's stage attire and theatrical movements became more diverse, and he started partially shaving his head and wearing white makeup on his face with dark makeup around his eyes. For the tour that produced the *Genesis Live* (1973) album, his attire included flowing robes, white gloves, and a large collar that suggested a flower (a reference to Narcissus in "Supper's Ready," as well as a crown of thorns for the section about "a new Jerusalem"). For the performance of "Supper's Ready," he wore the flowing robes at the beginning of the piece and by the end he wore a headdress resembling a series of angular boxes. Gabriel's stage outfits for this tour also included Britannia for "Selling England by the Pound." For most songs, however, Gabriel wore a black body suit; by 1973, the athleticism in his stage movements had increased markedly since the early Genesis tours. By the time of *The Lamb Lies Down on Broadway* tour of 1975, which featured the band playing a complete version of the double album of the same name, Gabriel had several costume changes ranging from a leather jacket (reflecting the narration in the lyrics relating to New York, various colors of body paints, and the grotesque "Slipperman" costume from the songs "The Slipperman" (with its opening line "I wandered lonely as a cloud" borrowed from William Wordsworth [1770–1850], who wrote the line in his poem "Daffodils" in 1802) and "A Visit to the Doktor" in which Gabriel refers to "the colony of Slippermen."

Gabriel left Genesis after this tour to pursue a solo career, and his videos began winning awards due to their play on MTV in the 1980s. Although his personal stage attire remained relatively normal in his solo concerts, his stage sets became more grandiose, and by the time of his collaborations with Canadian stage designer Robert Lepage in the early 1990s and his work in the 2000s with British architectural designer Mark Fisher, his concert staging became as important a factor to the "Gabriel experience" as his music. For his *Secret World* tour in 1993, his staging required "nine trucks hauling sixty feet of conveyor belt, two stages, an eight-foot tree, a red British telephone box, giant heads, fifty-eight crew and a band party of twelve, performing thirty-six shows in thirty-two different cities in forty-nine days."[1]

Gabriel's staging, however complex and sophisticated, could have been achieved only because of his overall commercial success, yet the notion of "spectacle" had been present, not just in progressive rock of the 1970s and onward, but also in areas such as glam rock in the same 1970s period.

DAVID AND ZIGGY

David Bowie became "Ziggy Stardust" as a stage persona in 1972. *The Rise and Fall of Ziggy Stardust and the Spiders from Mars* was Bowie's fifth album and, as with most of his albums before (such as *Hunky Dory* [1971]) and after *Ziggy Stardust*, it embodies Bowie's concept of himself as an actor as well as a rock singer, a mind-set that attracted media criticism at the time. Nevertheless, Bowie's Ziggy persona involved a stage projection of androgyny in terms of stage makeup and stage dress. His stage imagery was also adopted by his band members as Bowie unfolded a story of an alien being who has come to Earth to provide hope in the last years of Earth's existence. In doing so, the being indulges in sexual promiscuity and drug use. Bowie's stage act contained simulated sexual acts that were also performed, surprisingly, on the

BBC's premier pop rock program, *Top of the Pops*, and its progressive rock-oriented program, *Sounds of the 70s*, performances that drew both praise and criticism from the media and from fans. Nevertheless, the album was hailed as the thirty-fifth greatest album of all time by *Rolling Stone* magazine in 2012.[2]

Despite Bowie's attention to his own and his band's stage image and stage act, there were no specific stage props, further supporting his desire to be regarded as an actor as well as a rock performer. As Shelton Waldrep notes:

> The self-consciousness of his performances, which call attention to themselves as performances, threads through his work and unites his music as visual art. As Bowie himself said in the early seventies, he is at heart an actor, one who is playing a role whether it is before the microphone, on the stage, or before a camera. . . . That is to say, Bowie eschews the usual dictates of rock as purely a commodity that can control its form, content, and distribution in favour of an older Romantic idea that a popular form can be treated like "high" art.[3]

In a conversation in the 1970s, post-Genesis Gabriel told me that during his own performances, he adopted the same "actor" philosophy, partly because of his stage fright.[4]

Several of my interviewees have been, and still are, fans of Bowie's music and continual personal reinventions throughout his career (Steven Wilson was probably the most enthusiastic about Bowie's work). Despite some early singles being arguably borderline progressive, such as "Space Oddity," "John, I'm Only Dancing," and "Fashion" (which features King Crimson's Robert Fripp) and the fact that Rick Wakeman performed on several of his recordings, I would not put Bowie into a stylistic pigeonhole that labelled him as "progressive." However, the notions of visual creativity and conceptuality ran strongly through his glam period prior to his next period of self-reinvention, making his work in the 1970s a glam parallel to progressive rock.

One could also include Alice Cooper's "horror"-themed stage productions, which straddle a number of genres that include theatrical stage production and rock music performance. His songs fall into the album-oriented rock category, with songs constructed to garner radio airplay, and his horror stage themes have become a staple of his performances for several decades. That said, more recent Alice Cooper concerts include a number of macabre stage props that might move him into the descriptor of "conceptuality."

RICK WAKEMAN'S LIVE PERFORMANCES OUTSIDE YES

"Conceptuality" can easily be applied to keyboard player Rick Wakeman's work outside his session work for a wide variety of performers, including Bowie and Elton John over four decades, the Strawbs, and Yes and its spinoff bands. He has recorded about fourteen solo projects (at the time of this writing), and most have been commercial successes, despite being a working member of Yes and other bands during the creation of some of them. The three main solo projects for which Wakeman has received acclaim in the 1970s are *The Six Wives of Henry VIII* (1973), *Journey to the Centre of the Earth* (1974), and *The Myths and Legends of King Arthur and the Knights of the Round Table* (1975), although *1984* (1981) was his most commercially successful solo album. In terms of spectacle, the two albums from 1974 and 1975 are worthy of discussion, however. *Journey to the Centre of the Earth*, based on the Jules Verne science fiction novel, was recorded while Wakeman was still a member of Yes, after the band had finished recording *Tales from Topographic Oceans* and were on a break from touring. Wakeman's record label, A&M Records (Yes were signed to Atlantic Records, which often caused contractual problems for Wakeman), were wary of the cost of recording the album, for which Wakeman needed to hire orchestrators, a conductor, the London Symphony Orchestra, the English Chamber Choir, a narrator (actor David Hemmings), and a rock band. To make the album financially viable, the record company decided on a live recording of two performances of the work at the Royal Festival Hall but were unaware that the orchestra would have to be paid for both concerts under British Musicians' Union rules. It was decided that only the second concert would be recorded, which was a risk, though the process went relatively smoothly, apart from some small technical issues. Because of the high cost of the project, Wakeman sold some of his property and remortgaged his house. The album was registered multiplatinum within weeks of release, and Wakeman received an Ivor Novello award and a Grammy award for it. Twentieth Century Fox, the movie company that made the film of the novel in

1959, gave permission for the use of projections of the cave sequences from the film (the original music for the film was composed by Bernard Herrmann).

As a spectacle involving a prominent rock musician, a band, and an orchestra, this was not quite an original undertaking, however. Deep Purple had recorded Jon Lord's *Concerto for Group and Orchestra* at a live concert at the Royal Albert Hall in 1969 with the Royal Philharmonic Orchestra conducted by Malcolm Arnold. This concert received mixed reviews and, though Arnold praised Lord's composition and Deep Purple's musicianship, guitarist Ritchie Blackmore was scathing of the entire piece and felt unworthy to be playing with an orchestra.[5] As a member of the audience at the concert in 1969, I felt that although some sections worked cohesively between the orchestra and group, at times some members of Deep Purple looked almost apathetic.

Wakeman's concert, however, demonstrated that it was possible to combine all of his components—orchestral, choral, progressive rock, and visual projections—and it would set the presentation standard for progressive rock and indeed other rock performances in the future. Michael Kamen's work with Metallica and the San Francisco Symphony Orchestra, the Moody Blues' use of orchestras worldwide, and Roger Water's production of *The Wall* were other examples.

Wakeman's next undertaking would, however, exceed the visual production values of *Journey to the Centre of the Earth*. Having released three solo projects in three consecutive years, as well as presenting the second as a production that included many musicians and visual projections as a live spectacle that also produced a live recording, Wakeman took *The Myths and Legends of King Arthur and the Knights of the Round Table* even further. By this time, however, critical reviews regarded this type of production as excessive, a prediction, perhaps, of the genre that would follow. Using a different orchestra, the same choir, and the same rock band, Wakeman toured the production around the world with one notable difference from his two previous productions: Wakeman presented the show for three nights at Wembley Arena on ice. This part of the tour lost money, but the album was registered gold worldwide.

One problem on the 1975 recording was that the entire piece was too long for the vinyl LPs of the time (see the interview with David

Glasser) and certain sections had to be removed but were replaced when the work was rerecorded in 2016.

PINK FLOYD, THE WHO, AND LIGHTS

Both Pink Floyd and the Who continued to increase the elaborate staging of their concerts, and their use of laser technology became more sophisticated as lighting technologies advanced. Again, presenting a concert that was as stimulating visually as it was musically is limited to the domain of bands established and commercially viable enough to afford it. Bands such as Pink Floyd and the Who, however, have always attracted large audiences as they played world tours and can afford the additional production costs. There is also the aesthetic issue bands must take into consideration: the music highlighted and supported by a lighting display means that audiences associate what they see with what they hear. The Who have used a laser show since the late 1970s and have always been at the forefront of laser technology. Pink Floyd's own philosophy is to present a concert as a visual experience, which is more interesting than simply watching a group of people playing on stage. This philosophy has continued in David Gilmour's solo performances during the 2000s with the use of even more lasers and lighting technologies, as well as a central circular projection that highlights Gilmour and members of his band. In this way, audience members have the choice of being absorbed by the entire visual experience or focusing on Gilmour and the many celebrities who appear with him as guests (in the early 2000s these guests have included Stephen Stills, David Crosby, David Bowie, Phil Manzanera [Roxy Music], and Robert Wyatt [Soft Machine]).

RAMMSTEIN AND ROCK THEATER

From a European perspective, Rammstein is a band originally from East Germany, and which is slightly more difficult to define. Deena Weinstein terms the band "industrial dance metal" melded with thrash metal, though her description dates to when the band formed in the 1990s.[6] Like most of the bands already discussed, Rammstein's production aesthetic has increased parallel to their increasing commercial success. The band is commonly referred to as *"neue Deutsche Härte"* (new German hardness), but there are, however, several aspects that could make them borderline progressive rock in their performances since 2005, given the popularity of progressive rock that has lasted in Europe.

Although musical virtuosity places the band in the extreme metal category (with the use of low guitar tunings and relatively uncomplicated music), the band's sound production values are extremely high, which Allan F. Moore maintains is an essential component of progressive rock.[7] What also makes the band stand out from other bands performing in a saturated rock market and pushes them toward the progressive category is their reworking of German literature (for example, by Johann Wolfgang von Goethe [1749–1832] in their song "Dalai Lama" and by Heinrich Hoffman [1809–1894] in their song "Hilf Mir"). The band also address distasteful and often questionable German social issues as a form of parody that very few bands would include in their song lyrics. In doing so, they are influenced by the works of early-twentieth-century German impressionist poets such as Gottfried Benn (1886–1956) and Georg Heym (1887–1912), both of whom wrote about death, medical procedures, and decay. Rammstein's vocalist invariably sings in German with only a few exceptions (English, Spanish, and Russian). His broad vocal range enables him to move between bass baritone to the high registers of singers from early-twentieth-century German comedy cabaret, such as Frank Wedekind (1864–1918) and the singers used by Bertolt Brecht (1898–1956) and Kurt Weill (1900–1950) in their production of *The Threepenny Opera* (*Die Dreigroschenoper*) (1928). John Willet calls this cabaret vocal technique "gestic speaking."[8] Rammstein's lyrical content is credited to all band members, displaying knowledge of German literature spanning approximately two centuries, thus making the band comparable to many progressive rock bands who have used literature in their songs. All of the above allusions to "Germanness" have been achieved without any references to National Socialism and twentieth-century conflicts, which the band mostly avoids despite having their music dubbed onto German war films that are easily available on YouTube.

Visually, the band's live performances are theatrical and almost circuslike. Theatricality in German rock music has a legacy of more than four decades, two of its progenitors being Udo Lindenberg and Nina

Hagen.[9] Rammstein's performances since the late 1990s have, however, surpassed many successful rock bands, especially in Europe, in terms of visual production values. The band's performance at the Wuhlheide Festival in Berlin in 1998 began with flaming torches illuminating a large red curtain that covered the stage. The curtain dropped, and each member remained completely still, staring into the distance in statue-like poses individually illuminated by spotlights, juxtaposing a neoclassical image with the circuslike image presented by the vocalist, who was lowered to the stage on a trapeze. The silver clothing worn by the band was attached to plastic tubes and foam rubber sections. Some members wore silver contact lenses, and all wore silver makeup, giving an overall futuristic or robotic impression and perhaps drawing on the mechanical kinetic constructivism of Fritz Lang's film *Metropolis* (1927).

The tour that produced the *Völkerball (People's Ball)* DVD and album in 2006 took stage presentation even further, suggesting that audience expectations grow after each concert experience. By this time, band members had qualified as pyrotechnicians, and some songs featured the onstage use of flamethrowers. One such song is "Mien Teil," one of the band's songs that uses a salacious event as subject matter. The lyrics concern a murder in 2002 in which the murderer placed an online advertisement for a volunteer who wished to be slaughtered and eaten. A person volunteered, and the murderer did indeed eat him. Although the recording features all of Till Lindemann's vocal techniques, the version performed live for the DVD was somewhere between a horror movie and black comedy. The vocalist was dressed as a blood-spattered chef, whose microphone was taped to a large knife. There was an extremely large cooking pot onstage, inside which was the keyboard player. In the middle of the song, all stage lighting was switched off while the vocalist used a flamethrower to "cook" the keyboard player, much to the delight of the audience. In another song, "Feuer Frei," all band members left the stage except the keyboard player, who continued to play a simple, single-note melody. After about a minute, the rest of the band returned wearing flame-throwing headpieces that simultaneously created columns of fire above the band as they played the end of the song.

The stage set for this tour leaned even further toward the 1920s German mechanical kinetic constructivist style that was used in both theater and film at the time. The main structure central to the set had similarities to the demonic machine in Metropolis, including flickering lights similar to small lightning bolts reminiscent of Frankenstein's laboratory in James Whale's film *Frankenstein* (1931). The drummer was seated on top of this structure while band members entered the stage area through a central, circular portal. On this tour, band attire was distinctly Tyrolean, with a mixture of lederhosen, Tyrolean hats, and traditional eighteenth- and nineteenth-century clothing. The keyboard player often wore a German World War II military helmet, something that has been forbidden in Germany for many years.[10]

In videos, the visual production values also remain high. The song "Seemann" is filmed initially in monochrome before changing to color and features the band around the bow of a stationary, life-sized model of a ship amid wooden "waves" modelled in the shape of ripples, which were moved side by side to give the impression of moving water. This method is how sea scenes were created in Renaissance theater. The song "Amerika" (sung mostly in English) has the band in Apollo-era spacesuits in a studio setting of the moon's surface. The lyrics are critical of what they perceive as U.S. globalization of culture, although their own move to capitalism after reunification in 1990 has meant that the band has now become a successful commercial entity signed to the Universal Music Group. This business connection makes the views expressed in the song somewhat contradictory and perhaps hypocritical. Nevertheless, in another more recent video to promote the song "Mein Land," the band spoofs the Beach Boys and 1960s television beach culture. In short, whatever the band's political views, the audience's visual experience both live and in videos is as important to them as the high production values of their recordings as they promote a new, phoenix-like Germany with no references to negative events that occurred during the twentieth century.[11]

In conclusion, a final comment from Jakko Jakszyk of King Crimson, a band once at the forefront of experimental lighting, sums up an alternative, contemporary view about the presentation of progressive rock. When asked about how King Crimson play live nowadays, Jakszyk said:

> When we come onto the stage, the lights come up and there is no [special] lighting. . . . There's one lighting cue in the whole set, and that's the second half of "Starless [and Bible Black]." The lights slowly change till the whole stage is bathed in red. Up until that point, they're just working lights; we come on like an orchestra. So, the

house lights go down, and there's some working lights, and we walk on and we play and we play for two-and-a-bit hours until we get to "Starless," and then at the end of "Starless," all the lights go red, and that's the only lighting cue of the whole evening. Very different to most people. Robert's [Fripp] thing is there are seven guys up here playing interesting and at times challenging music, I think that's enough. We don't need the distraction of lights or films. . . . People should be interested enough to watch that. That's his take on it.[12]

A reason for this is possibly that King Crimson's audience has always expected an extremely high level of musicianship, with presentation perhaps a secondary consideration, whereas the enormity and extravagance of Rammstein's stage presentation makes up for a simpler approach to their musicianship.

The next chapter discusses bands that formed in the first era of progressive rock during the late 1960s through the 1970s and that are still performing nowadays alongside the postprogressive bands already discussed, which mostly formed in the late 1980s and continued into the 2000s. Some have continued performing since their formation, while others have re-formed after being involved with other bands and projects.

7

NEW LIFE

Reuniting for Renewed Success

In the 1990s and 2000s, progressive rock went through what might be termed a revival that was, to an extent, Eurocentric, though with contributions from the progressive metal styles emerging from Scandinavia. Several progressive bands had remained together since their formation, albeit with a number of breaks, and others re-formed after longer periods of inactivity. In all cases, however, they enjoyed a new period of commercial success among preexisting, as well as new, audiences. Descriptions of some of these reunions and elements of revivalism collected from some of the musicians who have discussed their personal experiences with me follow. These experiences differ according to each band's popularity after a hiatus from performing and each musician's professional circumstances.

PROGRESSIVE PIONEERS

After the punk era of the late 1970s, many bands in the progressive genre had, as previously stated, disbanded or changed style. For example, when one examines the two seminal British progressive folk-rock bands, Fairport Convention and Steeleye Span, both took a break at this time, yet re-formed within only a few years. Both bands had a firm following among a folk-oriented, progressive audience, and despite losing its record contract due to poor album sales, Fairport Convention carried on with well-attended live performances. Simon Nicol, a founding member and leader of the band, explained that Fairport Convention performed a number of "final" performances, the most significant being the main support act for Led Zeppelin at the Knebworth Festival in 1979. The band then played a definitive final performance the same evening in Cropredy village hall (a village in Oxfordshire), given that most members lived in the surrounding area.[1] In 1980, the band decided to perform a reunion gig in the same hall. This rekindled an interest in re-forming the band on a more permanent basis (though by doing so, bassist Dave Pegg simultaneously became a member of both Fairport Convention and Jethro Tull in the mid- to late 1980s). The Cropredy Festival quickly became an annual event attracting audiences in excess of twenty thousand each year.[2] Nowadays, the band has established its own management and record label and perform annual tours that promote new recordings.[3]

Steeleye Span had enjoyed commercial success in the mid-1970s with a folk pop crossover single produced by established pop producer Mike Batt, who was famous for composing music for a high profile children's television program. The single, "All around My Hat" (1975) was divisive among Steeleye Span's fan base, and the band was regarded as having "sold out" by its progressive and folk fans alike. With the loss of a large part of its fan base, the band was unable to withstand the punk period and disbanded in the late 1970s with members pursuing different solo projects. Like Fairport Convention, however, the band reunited in the early 1980s and have recorded and toured successfully since then, albeit with several changes in lineup. The band's latest lineup, performing since 2002, has been stable for some years and has several original members, including Maddy Prior, one of the band's original vocalists, who had at times collaborated with Jethro Tull (a further example of membership fluidity and mutual collaboration in progressive rock).[4]

COLOSSEUM

It would seem, therefore, that once musical chemistry forms a bond among certain musicians, there is often a lasting need to reestablish the

performances that were staple to a band's original formation and existence. The British progressive jazz-rock band Colosseum had a much
longer period of inactivity yet re-formed. Disbanding in 1971, all members were successful in other established bands, particularly guitarist
Clem Clempson, who enjoyed international success with Humble Pie.
In the 1990s, however, a reunion birthday party reignited the band's
interest in performing together. Clempson describes how this happened.

> The plan to get Colosseum together was formulated when we were
> all brought together by Jan Greenslade for a surprise birthday party
> for Dave's [Greenslade, the band's keyboard player] fiftieth in 1994.
> We hadn't seen each other for years; we had a great evening and
> joked about getting back together, but I was serious! Next morning, I
> called Jon [Hiseman, the band's founder and drummer], who said
> he'd had a lot of enquiries from promoters about whether we'd con-
> sider playing some shows. So we all met up again for a blow, loved
> every minute, and it was decided that we would play the Freiburg
> Music Festival in spring of 1995 and record it with a view to having a
> new CD available when we went on the road the following year. We
> had a great gig, although we weren't satisfied with much of the re-
> cording and subsequently planned a show at the E-Werk in Cologne,
> which would be recorded for a CD and DVD, and which of course is
> now available on YouTube. Our first reunion tour took place later
> that year.
>   We knew there was a lot of interest, but the scale of the demand
> was quite overwhelming; the combination of that demand from all
> over Europe and the incredible passion that we encountered from
> the fans who'd been waiting many years to see us play again, plus the
> fact that we had an absolute ball on the tour, led us to keep going for
> the next twenty years or so![5]

I had been working with various members of Colosseum during the
early 1990s in a spinoff band that at various times included Neil Hubbard (Roxy Music), Bob Weston (Fleetwood Mac), and Snowy White
(Thin Lizzy) on guitar. David Gilmour often played with the band, but
his commitments to the preparation and recording of *The Division Bell*
album (1994) were his main priority, so Clempson joined the band.
Also, Colosseum vocalist Chris Farlowe occasionally performed with
the band, as did Dick Heckstall-Smith. The spinoff band ended when

Clempson announced a "two-year reunion" for Colosseum that lasted twenty-one years, and thus his comments about the audience reaction reflect a situation that many progressive bands experienced.

ILLUSION/RENAISSANCE

To enable some progressive musicians to continue performing during the late 1970s and 1980s, many bands formed with extremely fluid memberships. I asked guitarist John Knightsbridge about how membership changed at the time and how re-forming had affected his career, given that Renaissance had disbanded but reunited with a new name, Illusion:

> Illusion was the original Renaissance band that reunited—at first with Keith Relf [former lead vocalist with the Yardbirds] with the plan to bring me in on lead guitar, but shortly after that he was electrocuted and died. The group decided to carry on and then Jim [Carty, former drummer with the Yardbirds] moved from drums to acoustic guitar and vocals. Another group had taken the name Renaissance, but there was still a lot of interest in the original group and a fair amount of product moved in the early days. As far as I could tell, there was a lot of friendship there from the sixties and the group re-signed with Island Records. With the arrival of punk rock, interest in progressive material waned! When the group got together again to record some more material I was living in the States and missed out.[6]

Despite his comments about the band's friendship (a common occurrence in progressive rock that was probably a result of mutual respect for musicianship) and its original name being used by another band (despite the original band's songs that became hits), Knightsbridge was able, like many progressive musicians, to establish a career essentially as a freelance guitarist. Knightsbridge went on to work with a number of bands that were popular in Europe and Scandinavia. In one particular band, he performed with Tony Fernandez, later to be Rick Wakeman's drummer, and Chas Cronk, the bassist from the Strawbs, a band that started Rick Wakeman's career before his tenure with Yes and that is still touring and recording with Fernandez on drums and Adam Wakeman (Rick's son) on keyboards. A fortuitous connection while writing for a music magazine led Knightsbridge to return to his original influences when he formed Ruthless Blues, a band that drew upon some of the best progressive musicians in the United Kingdom, including Fernandez (as stated, many progressive guitarists were highly influenced by the blues). This band formed in the early 1980s and lasted into the 2000s, playing loud blues covers with the technical mastery of progressive rock, and established a large following among progressive rock fans unaware of the band members' earlier reputations. The band thus attracted a younger audience that were experiencing blues for the first time, albeit played by Europeans.

10CC

Other musicians and bands had problematic legal issues such as name ownership and the consequences of performing an established repertoire after disbanding, with members forming new bands that performed the same material. Rick Fenn, the guitarist of progressive pop band 10cc, described the consequences of tensions and finally a split between the band's two principal songwriters.

> Back in October '83, we really did stop for pretty much ten years. Apart from a couple of TVs [shows] in '91 and again in '92 (each with various drummers/keyboard players) we didn't tour till March '93 in Japan. Of the '83 band, other than Graham and Eric, of course, only Stuart Tosh [the 10cc drummer following Paul Burgess] and I were involved, and though it was great to play the music again and work with Steve Piggot and Gary Wallis [session musicians from outside the original band], there was friction between Eric and Graham that hung like a cloud and actually blew up into a cyclonic storm during the U.K. tour, which was very unpleasant. And though we had clearly retained much of our popularity, the houses weren't as full as they had been ten years before. To be honest, for me personally, I had had a very, very busy ten years touring, writing, and recording. In fact, I still was very busy with lots of musical projects. I'd done a lot of stuff with Graham over that time anyway, but it was lovely to work with Eric again in spite of the tensions with Graham. I like Eric very much but I have to say that I love the current Mk III band [the current band] and I don't miss those tensions at all. . . . So there you have it. We never really stopped after Eric—just sort of morphed.[7]

Legalities did not prevent part of the band from performing the previously established repertoire, but unable to use the band's name, Fenn describes the difficulties they encountered, much like the legal difficulties experienced by members of Pink Floyd for similar reasons already discussed.

> After Eric Stewart's last 10cc gig, which was the Esbjerg festival in Denmark in June '95, activity (without him) didn't stop for long but it took various forms. Only two months later we did a TV show as the Graham Gouldman Band. In '97 we started a series of acoustic gigs in Graham's name and in various lineups, which included for the first time Mick Wilson [a vocalist and guitarist performing Stewart's role], who has been in the band since July '97. This gradually morphed into an electric band, still in GG's [Graham Gouldman's] name, but we did actually appear on the National Lottery TV show as 10cc in March '99, doing "Dreadlock Holiday," and this was the first time Paul Burgess was back in the fold since July '83. In spite of that, we did a few more electric gigs as the GG band until July '99, when we did our first festival gig using the epithet "Graham Gouldman's 10cc." Or at least I think that was how it was presented—it's hard to remember exactly, as it was a slow process of dipping our toes in the water and we were always up against the promoters' often unscrupulous efforts to augment the name 10cc in preference to Graham's. But our attempts to prefix the 10cc name with Graham's went on until at least 2006. You may remember our 2006 New Zealand tour being burdened, and the business consequently seriously diminished, by this. In fact, I think it was probably that tour, where the commercial consequences of the confusing name showed themselves to be so damaging, that prompted us to start using the name 10cc. Some promoters were using it anyway, in spite of contracts preventing them, and we appeared to be getting away with it, so by then the "Graham Gouldman" prefix was officially dropped.[8]

Although legal problems beset some bands' attempts to retain their names and thus their audiences, other progressive musicians had already established successful solo careers, having left bands in which they made their reputations. The next section explains how a much more amicable split enabled all members of a band to benefit from an individual's own new career.

STEVE HACKETT

Steve Hackett, the former guitarist with Genesis, left the band in 1977, although there were a handful of Genesis reunions in the years that followed, as well as members of Genesis occasionally performing with Hackett's band. In this instance, the animosity described by some of the interviewees was never an issue. Hackett has released more than twenty solo albums during the years after his departure from Genesis and has never stopped performing. Both bassist and Chapman stick player Nick Beggs and drummer Gary O'Toole have performed as Hackett's rhythm section for several years. O'Toole described how he was asked to join Hackett's band:

> I saw Steve Hackett for the first time at the Venue in Victoria [London]. I remember thinking "damn, how do you play this? It's completely off the wall!" I was aware of Steve but hadn't really listened to his stuff, although I recall thinking I should give it a shot at some point as the drums were so challenging. I was still deeply into Billy Cobham [former Mahavishnu drummer]. When I started with Steve, I had heard the stuff and knew I should practice like mad, so I did. He hired a studio for a week to rehearse the stuff. "Ready?" I asked, and counted off the first song that Steve was concerned we would have to run lots. At the end of the first run, through, it was nailed! An impromptu tea break was called as he was so relieved. At one point I had songs to sing, which were mainly backing vocals, but gradually he asked me to do more. I agreed and he was surprised I can manage it. We were running "Watcher of the Skies," but solely as an instrumental.[9]

Once O'Toole had established that he could sing while playing drums, Hackett started to include more early Genesis (Gabriel-era) songs in the live set. O'Toole described how he had to persuade Hackett to let him sing them, often with criticism from Hackett's record company:

> I said to Steve, "I can sing it, too," at which point he informed me it couldn't be done according to our great mate, the lovely John Wetton [the progressive bassist with the prolific progressive rock career described earlier]. I said "Look, let's run it, you don't like it, we do it your way again." So I became the lead singer for quite a few tunes,

"Watcher of the Skies," "Carpet Crawlers," "Firth of Fifth," and "Blood on the Rooftops." I adored singing, but it was suggested I might come down the front and present the show, etcetera. I agreed but the record company got involved and ruined that for me. Nad [Nad Sylvan, the current band vocalist] is a nice man and a great singer, so life moves on. Like I said to Steve, "I don't like the decision, but it's your name on that can of beans and not mine!"

Don't get me wrong here, I am not bitter about it, this is just the way the industry toys with us, as you well know, mate!

The material began as solely Steve's stuff but he had more and more demands to do Genesis stuff, so we gradually got to the point where we did two and a half years of "Genesis Revisited" shows. Now they insist on Genesis material but it's all good, and Steve is a pro![10]

The fact that Hackett maintained his earlier reputation as the lead guitarist with Genesis despite his success as a solo artist is testament to his early Genesis legacy. As with 10cc, performing without the complete band (albeit with occasional performances with various Genesis members) did not matter to the large audiences Hackett attracted, given the musical prowess of his band members and their own reputations. Both Beggs and O'Toole remarked to me that Hackett's own material is extremely complex and, though he never calls it progressive and in fact dislikes the term, it retains the tropes of that descriptor.

KING CRIMSON

Having interviewed bassist and Chapman stick player Tony Levin, who has been a member of King Crimson since 1981, it became apparent that a second interview with a more recent addition to the band would be useful in any investigation into band reunions. I therefore discussed the formation of the latest incarnation of the band with guitarist and vocalist Jakko Jakszyk. Jakszyk, who had worked with Robert Fripp in 2011 on the album *A Scarcity of Miracles*, which also featured other members of the future King Crimson, including drummer Gavin Harrison (formerly Steven Wilson's drummer), Tony Levin, and saxophonist Mel Collins, a member of King Crimson from 1970 to 1974. Jakszyk describes how the recording occurred and how the album lineup became the current King Crimson:

> the first thing really was he [Fripp] invited me down to a DGM [Discipline Global Mobile, King Crimson's own management company]. . . . They've got an office down in Wiltshire. They're in a little village called Broad Chalke. That's where the organization's run from, that's where the management is, and they've got a recording facility. So, a very humble recording facility and he [Fripp] asked me down to improvise with him because he had this idea about . . . he would ask different people to come down and improvise and see what happens. I know he did it with one other guitar player and with me and then it stopped, really, then he just decided, "Oh, actually I quite like this." We sat in a room, he had all that looping stuff going and the soundscape effect, and we spent a day just both playing live and recording it all, and at the end of the day, he gave me the hard drive and said, "Why don't you take this away with you?" and I said, "And do what?" He said, "I don't know."[11]

This statement is similar to that made by Levin about the King Crimson lineup that formed in 1981 during the "Discipline" period. Fripp's modus operandi seems to be to find musicians with whom he has a musical rapport and then jam with them. Having recorded whatever has been played, he then allows musicians to add their own ideas, and these are reinterpreted into new versions of the band. Significantly, Fripp had invited a member of the second King Crimson lineup from the 1970s, Mel Collins, who enabled the band to return to some of the material from that period.

This new album, however, was not the immediate starting point of a new King Crimson lineup. As with previous lineups, the formation of the band often starts with a Fripp project outside the main band. Jakszyk describes how the album progressed.

> So, I went away and I created the songs on top of it and parts of that eventually became [the] album called *A Scarcity of Miracles* and on that [Fripp] said, "Let's get Mel to play on it," because he loves Mel's playing and it was an excuse to work with Mel in a way that, well, he hadn't done since the seventies. And then I've recorded, I've used fake drums, and I played the bass myself, and I said, "Well, you need to get real bass on top of this and real drums. Can we use Gavin [Harrison]?" And he said, "Yeah, why don't we use Tony [Levin]?" So, I think that was the genesis of it. We've kind of got this new lineup here, and there was talk and emails flying around about what

he [Fripp] was provisionally calling "Project Seven," with a view to doing some live stuff with basically that lineup. And then nothing happened. . . . Well, anyway, eventually that came out and then he told me he has this thing—you know, where he says he has a vision— he suddenly had a vision of three drummers. And Bill Rieflin [keyboard player for King Crimson] is a friend of his and they've worked in a group called "Slow Music," which is an improvised thing with [French avant garde composer] Hector Zazou. So, there's Robert's take on it about having this vision and then there's the practical history which locks in with that. So, he just phoned us all up and said, "I'm thinking of re-forming King Crimson with three drummers and Mel, and would you like to be the lead singer and second guitar player?" [12]

From Jakszyk's comprehensive description, it seems that there is a method Fripp uses that is borne not only from his creativity, but also from a form of fluid networking among musicians with whom he has worked in the past and new musicians whose work he admires. Fripp is not alone in this, given the fluidity of progressive rock band membership for more than four decades.

To conclude, the reasons for which progressive rock bands reform—either after short breaks or after decades—obviously vary, but several attributes are common to all of the bands described in this chapter. They include the enjoyment of musical performance at virtuosic levels, the curiosity of new musical creations, and the mutual admiration among these musicians that always remains, sometimes even under acrimonious circumstances. Such is the influence of some of these earlier bands that more recent bands still draw on their work for inspiration. The next chapter discusses what progressive rock has become in the new millennium and how some bands and musicians eschew the term. Others still use it as a means of allying what they perform with the music from the late 1960s and 1970s that was called "progressive" and "underground." One must also consider how the music is accessed by its audience. From information mostly gleaned from interviews, it seems that a return to pre-digitization and the reissues of vinyl, albeit with highly sophisticated technological reproduction, has given the genre a further boost in popularity.

8

POSTPROG

A New Struggle for Definition

In an attempt to define what progressive rock has become in the new millennium, it is worth revisiting its origins, despite the fact that the word "progressive" is still in use as a contemporary description among performers and audiences. Technology played a major role in the emergence of the musical style (along with other aspects such as virtuosity, conceptuality, curiosity, etc.), and its presence is still apparent. In regard to terminology, there seems to be a differing viewpoint among performers and a broad range of listeners. The remix culture has had a profound effect on progressive rock, but is it an era or a current and changing style? Therefore, the problematic issue mainly lies in how the music is described by individual performers or audience members.

It is significant that sales of vinyl recordings rose more than 53 percent in 2016 as record audiences turned away from streaming (downloading highly compressed music).[1] From the perspective of use of technology and the return of vinyl as a preferred format among perfectionist audience members (particularly progressive, jazz, and classical), my interview with Steven Wilson indicated that many of the established performers for whom he produced surround 5.1 remixes never thought of themselves as "progressive." Allen Ginsberg's term "underground" seems to be their word of choice, and it was what the BBC disc jockey John Peel called the music in the late 1960s and the 1970s (after which period he championed more alternative music styles). It is therefore noteworthy that some of the more recent bands (by which I mean bands that have formed during the late twentieth century and during the new millennium) still have elements of the earliest progressive rock styles and also utilize new technologies that have emerged during the age of digitization. It is also significant that the analog equipment used in the 1960s and 1970s often commands premium secondhand prices, despite the digital copies of these effects being available on industry-standard recording software products. Wilson's views, however, oppose purist opinions:

> I think, nowadays, digital technology has pretty much caught up with analog. The resolution we can work out now, the tools that we have, the emulations of the old analog equipment is phenomenal, absolutely phenomenal. And I know there will always be purists who will say, "Well, there's a certain kind of distortion and compression you got from working through analog desks." That's true, but let's say this. If these projects had to be done on analog, they wouldn't happen, because you're talking about doing 5.1 mixes for a few thousand dollars, a few thousand pounds. That would buy you like a day in a 5.1 analog studio. So, they have to be done digitally, is the answer.[2]

This is particularly apparent in early progressive rock rereleases and in even more recent new releases. As previously stated, David Glasser has been remastering the entire Grateful Dead back catalog for several years in 5.1 surround sound, CD, and for vinyl. These collections usually sell out in days, suggesting that the vinyl legacy is still a question of aural quality and that the MP3 format is not of a high enough quality to the connoisseur. The issue of aural quality is always paramount to the progressive rock audience, in which connoisseurship is common. Glasser's own method of remastering vinyl or for digital is as follows: "[I] mastered from the original master tapes in Airshow Studio C, Boulder, Colorado. Transfers were done at 192kHz/24 bit from an Ampex ATR with Plangent replay electronics to a Prism ADA-8XR A/D converter into a soundBlade workstation. The studio, designed by Sam Berkow, has Dunlavy SC-V loudspeakers driven by Ayre Acoustic amps."[3]

Though Glasser is discussing remastering for a variety of formats, his statement means that, in order to reproduce recordings made in the 1970s for vinyl release, modern technologies will improve what was once at the forefront of recording technology. And, as previously stated, progressive rock has always been driven by technological advances. This concept has enabled progressive rock bands to reissue their back catalogs in vinyl and other formats. Wilson has strong views on this phenomenon, given his own remix experience.

> I'm from the last generation that discovered music through vinyl, because [for] the next generation after me, CD was dominant. And so, growing up in the '80s was the last generation that was still buying records on vinyl. And for me, it is a very tactile experience. Putting a record on, lowering the needle. One of the things about vinyl, you can even see the music. You can see, "Oh, there's a quiet section coming up." You can see the grooves get a bit lighter. And, "Oh, there's a long track coming up." It's something very magical and romantic about that very tactile experience of taking the vinyl out of the record. It's like film fanatics talk about lacing projectors and watching a Super 8 film. Something almost sensual about that, romantic about that. And it's the same with vinyl. And CD began to erode that, although I do think there are ways to make the CD experience more romantic. And, of course, we've seen a massive increase in this concept of deluxe additions [rereleases of back catalogs].[4]

These statements indicate that although Wilson dislikes the term "progressive," he is au fait with both old and new technologies and old and new progressive performance styles. If the term was to be used to describe a musical style in a state of constant progression rather than as a descriptor for a musical period, the term might not be problematic. This is especially so as he is aware that a completely new mix on a rerelease might not be commercial. It is worth noting that Wilson has won three awards in the U.K. *Prog* magazine (the magazine that promoted the annual Progressive Music Awards between 2012 and 2016). These awards included a Guiding Light award (2012), a Storm Thorgerson Grand Design award for *Hand.Cannot.Erase*, and a Best Album award for the same album (2015). It would seem that Wilson's ability to embrace both old and the new, both musically and technologically, is the reason for his prolific success.

From a musical perspective, other musicians interviewed were not concerned by a descriptor, preferring to use other terms and not returning to their—or any other bands'—earlier roots. For example, Jakko Jakszyk of King Crimson countered Wilson's views about how music is defined with the following statement:

> He's been on the front page of *Prog* magazine innumerable times, but there you go, bless him. Well, Robert's [Fripp] the same; Robert won't entertain the word "prog." I don't give a fuck really, it's all music and people can call it what they want. And I understand that, you know, if people want to put it in a virtual section, then what the hell, I don't care. You know, call it what you like. I mean it wasn't called prog when I was a kid, it was called "underground."[5]

Although "progressive" rock music at times can be defined within a number of genres, Paul Hegarty and Martin Halliwell describe what they regard as "neoprog" that emerged in the 1980s and that may have been a reaction to 1970s progressive rock. They describe this music as "ambient music, forms of jazz, and *krautrock*, New York art rock, and electronic music."[6] For them, however, "postprogressive" is a style that emerged from the "persistence of progressive rock and it is not a synonym for 'postmodern.'" Within this more recent stylistic development, they include Mars Volta, Radiohead, Muse, and Spock's Beard.[7] Their inclusion of bands such as Ride and My Bloody Valentine is, however, dubious, as are their views move without direction at times discussing what they refer to as "indie" bands (despite most having achieved commercial success) being progressive. Most of the examples they provide, however, were most popular in the 1980s and 1990s. More significantly, they state that postprogressive rock "starts from a different place from classic [*sic*] progressive rock of the 1970s"; instead, they argue that postprogressive rock is not a "mid-point between progressive rock and its successor styles" but a "new fusion," a description I support.[8] This view is also supported by many current progressive musicians, although Hegarty and Halliwell stop short (due to their 2011 publication date) of acknowledging developments in new (post?) progressive rock during the last six years. It is this concept of a fusion of styles with rock music that is the defining descriptor that easily provides an identity for a style that may have originated in the late 1960s and early 1970s but that has emerged in the new millennium with the elements that made it attract a curious audience still intact.

Whatever an individual artist or band wants to call the music, there comes a point, as Jakszyk points out in his earlier statement, when one can label the music however one likes. Wilson's use of the term "curiosity" also comes to mind as an integral component of what might be termed "experimental fusion" instead of "progressive," thus leaving composers and performers to decide where they want to go musically. From Jakszyk's description of his initial experiences when he joined King Crimson, there was no blueprint beyond Fripp's vision of an unusual combination of musicians. Consequently, the term "postprogressive" limits what the music has become as musicians' curiosity and experimentation have kept the style in a more or less continual state of development, thus making it "progressive" in the true sense of the word rather than limiting it to an era that requires the prefix "post" to separate one specific phase from another. Although some of the more contemporary bands appropriate elements from earlier bands, the "progression" in the music remains apparent. In a discussion about how the current King Crimson lineup prepares for touring and recording, Jakszyk explained how Robert Fripp is still experimenting with his guitar style and tuning and has been doing so since the 1980s: "[He uses what is called] new standard tuning. So, his bottom string is tuned to C. So, it goes C, G, E, D, A, E. I call that prog. People aren't afraid to say, 'Well, why should I tune my guitar this way and not that way?'"[9]

When asked about bands using seven- or eight-string guitars such as those used by Meshuggah and Animals As Leaders, he gave his views on the complexity of playing and singing in a band like King Crimson:

> I'm playing with six strings, I'm not buggering about with that [seven- and eight-string guitars]. It's hard enough as it is, mate. For instance, very shortly after coming back from the last tour, a couple of days later, Robert wrote a list of Crimson songs and said, "Jakko, can you sing any of these?" And I wrote back straightaway and said, "I can sing any of them, Robert. The problem occurs when I have to play your guitar part whilst I'm singing." So, the real challenge for me is some of the things I have to play and sing. In fact, we were writing one of the new pieces together, and because I demoed them up here [at Jakszyk's home studio], when he came back [to hear] one of the pieces we'd been working on, I played it back to him and he said, "What's going on in that chorus there?" And what was going on was I had deliberately written the guitar part I knew I could play and sing at the same time. He said, "No, no, I think it sounds much better if you're playing the cross-pick thing against me where I'm

playing it in . . ." And I gave an audible exhale of breath and said to
him, "You do know I have to play and sing this at the same bloody
time?" To which he said, "I know, it's marvelous. I don't know how
you do it." [10]

Fripp's obvious admiration for Jakszyk's ability to sing and play complex music demonstrates yet another example of the mutual admiration
for musicianship that exists among progressive rock musicians, though
one cannot ignore a hint of humor in Fripp's final statement. Jakzyk's
admiration for Fripp is obvious in the following statement: "It has its
daunting aspects for me [being the lead singer] but funnily enough, it
isn't so much that. It's the fact that the fan boy in me sits there and
Robert says, as he did before we even rehearsed the first time, when he
said, 'Oh, I'm thinking of maybe doing "Larks' Tongues in Aspic, part
one."' So, the fan boy in me thinks, 'Wow, amazing, how brilliant.'" [11]

It would be difficult, if not impossible, to find descriptors beyond
"progressive" and "underground" for what Jakszyk ably describes, despite the possibility of pigeonholing the music within a 1970s time
frame, which would be inaccurate. Internet searches have provided
descriptions such as the aforementioned contemporary term "progressive metal." This amount of titular variation indicates that there are
many bands combining metal with a combination of styles, a similar
phenomenon to the use of "jazz-rock," "folk-rock," and "classical rock"
in the 1970s, all of which were used without the use of the word "progressive"—the media's umbrella term for the entire genre. "Progressive
pop" is another term in use to describe some bands. The continued
inclusion of "progressive" in contemporary descriptions only reinforces
the term's usefulness, however, especially as the style has established
close ties with more sophisticated and complex metal than that of the
1970s and 1980s.

Although the bands from the 1970s have performed reunion tours
and recorded new live albums maintaining their original sonic identities
(doing otherwise would probably have alienated preexisting audiences,
given that the audiences would expect a nostalgic zeitgeist), the more
recent progressive bands, metal and otherwise, have the freedom to
explore—and break—new musical boundaries. The multiple styles apparent on all of the Animals As Leaders albums are an excellent illustra-
tion of musical versatility and open-mindedness among band members.
As described, the band easily switches between classical guitar styles

and jazz and then move into metal styles heavier than anything produced by Black Sabbath, Iron Maiden, and Metallica. The ability to
seamlessly move between such diverse styles, most often in the same
piece, is yet another long-lasting descriptor of progressive rock (listen to
pieces such as Yes' "Machine Messiah," Colosseum's "The Grass Is
Always Greener," 10cc's "I'm Mandy, Fly Me," and King Crimson's "In
the Court of the Crimson King," which have been discussed already, for
just a few examples). This stylistic ability therefore remains apparent
nowadays.

In addition, the notion that a piece of music should be confined by a
time limit (given that classical music is not) and a structure remains
outside the progressive mind-set. The progressive rock method of composition can be a preplanned structural arrangement or the result of
improvisation that remains spontaneous when played live or that yields
new ideas that are crafted into more structured arrangements in which
little or no improvisation takes place. Composition itself has also
changed with the development of new composition and programming
software. When I interviewed Nick Beggs and Steven Wilson, both said
that they were able to compose alone, easily, in a multitude of locations
because of portable technology. Although Wilson went back into his
studio upon the completion of the lengthy *Hand.Cannot.Erase.* tour to
start his next album, Beggs was actually composing music for his own
band, the Mute Gods, on a laptop computer in his hotel room while
performing on the tour for Wilson.

Conversely, the precision of Meshuggah and Tesseract's metrical
arrangements prevents any spontaneous stylistic move away from what
had been rehearsed. Both of these methods of composition and performance—pre-rehearsed and spontaneous—were becoming more common in the 1980s in the wake of bands such as Soft Machine and others
in the 1970s, and especially in King Crimson's 1980s "Discipline" period. Many other progressive bands, especially those that were or are
jazz-oriented, have followed both means of creating new music since
that time.

As the title of this chapter suggests, there remains a struggle for
definition as many "progressive rock'" musicians cannot agree on a single descriptor for the music they create. Although many refuse to be
pigeonholed into a formulaic style yet often use influences from progressive music's origins in the late 1960s and the 1970s (including virtu-

osity, complex composition, and the search for the re-creation of early musical sounds from modern technology), others use the progressive term because it identifies them as curious and experimental (like the music that was created four decades ago) yet still breaking barriers. In other words, the argument goes back to what has been suggested earlier: is "progressive" a period or a progression in the creation of new music?

From the majority of interviews carried out for this book and from discussions I have had with professional musicians working in complex, and what I have referred to as virtuosic areas of music during the last thirty to forty years, it seems that the notion of musical "progression" is more important to performers than adherence to a set time period. That said, and despite well-promoted and successful reunions, even members of established progressive bands have performed live in combinations that have included, in one example, former members of King Crimson, Genesis, Frank Zappa's band, Asia, and Weather Report, which played music from early 1970s progressive rock.[12] There is, therefore, an existing audience for the nostalgic zeitgeist as much as there is for the curiosity that leads to new fusions and combinations. It is the question of "where to now?" that, to an extent, steers and governs what progressive music has become since the 1990s. From an audience perspective, there are bands that fall into a number of stylistic categories under a broad "progressive" umbrella that largely depends on the views and tastes of the listener. The next chapter therefore examines, by use of anecdotes from interviewees for this book, a number of different methods of defining the music in an attempt to pinpoint what contemporary progressive rock may or may not have become in the first part of the new millennium and what its essential components might be.

9

CONCLUSION

Is Contemporary Progressive Rock Driven by
Musical "Progression"?

On a U.K. Channel 4 television program in 2004, composer and author
Howard Goodall asked which performers and composers might be re-
membered two hundred years in the future while listing composers
from the twentieth century who already have achieved legendary status.[1] He said he believed that by the mid-1960s, popular and classical
music had "collided" with each other to create a new musical "mainstream" while breaking away from music that academics call Western
art music (classical music). He implied that postwar modernism in classical music was at a low ebb by the 1960s. This provided an opportunity
for an amalgamation between popular music and classical music, since
both were easily assimilated, given what classical music was becoming
and the sophistication emerging in some rock and popular music. Although the program mainly discussed the Beatles, many of his descriptions of their musical evolution easily apply to progressive rock in general. Descriptions such as "an extraordinary, unprecedented melting
pot," "embraced new technologies with enthusiasm and imagination,"
"proving music could be both genuinely sophisticated and genuinely
popular," and "exhilarating inventiveness" were used to illustrate how
the Beatles approached their compositions, arrangements, and studio
performances. These descriptions fit their music and that of the em-
bryonic progressive rock bands that followed in the wake of *Sgt. Pepper*

(1967) and during the late 1960s and into the 1970s. Contemporary progressive rock has consistently evolved from these kinds of musical tropes during the last four decades. Borrowing Isaac Newton's statement that he learned by "standing on the shoulders of giants," one can often trace a lineage through these four decades or more of progressive rock, much like the evolution of classical music through several centuries.

The conceptuality described in an earlier chapter, which seems to be a remnant of the 1970s and 1980s, may no longer be as prevalent (except perhaps for Rammstein's circus-like parody and satire), yet there have been changes in audience reception for progressive rock in recent years. The stadium approach for established progressive bands, most often for those with a long musical legacy, will always encourage excitement and an enthusiastic audience response. Simon Frith, however, compares various styles of music that command different types of audience attention. For example, audience stillness at a classical concert is now matched by the same stillness at a jazz concert, which is unusual given that jazz had its origins in dance music. The same issue can easily be applied to folk music concerts that demand the same audience concentration.[2] Whereas the roots of rock music come from a meeting between country music and African American rhythm and blues, and both styles have the same potential for being dance music, progressive rock has moved, in many instances, closer to its classical and jazz counterparts mainly in the concert hall setting. Thus, the criticism leveled at the elitism of some early progressive bands that aspired to high art may well be valid still. Ultimately, it is for the audience to decide how a band is received. From Jakszyk's description of a modern King Crimson performance and other performances of a complex nature described earlier, it seems that progressive rock audience concentration is taken as a given, even with the air of excitement that inevitably accompanies it. A further audience-related issue is that of sound reproduction of recordings. Interviews with Steven Wilson, David Glasser, and Jakko Jakszyk have provided information about technological processes used in the reproduction of both old and new progressive rock recordings and their distribution in a number of advanced formats for new record labels. Progressive rock musicians therefore seem to use several options, depending on their current levels of success. Significantly, it should be noted that an older progressive rock audience may have the disposable income necessary for the acquisition of the theater sound system described by Glasser that is necessary to reproduce a 5.1 (or higher) surround sound remix.

Looking back at more than four decades of what is still most often referred to as "progressive rock," definitions—much like many forms of music—are often governed by periodicity (when styles either began or were most popular) or by their longevity and what I describe as "developmental progression." Some of the interviewees for this book eschew the term "progressive," as do the artists they perform with, whereas others use the term with no concern about its supposed potential for pigeonholing what they compose and perform. There were opinions expressed that, from a stylistic perspective, progressive rock is an ongoing progression in which musical styles are recycled, reworked, and taken into new areas. Certainly the descriptions provided in several interviews support this view. It is also obvious that making radical changes to existing repertoire potentially would be detrimental to popularity for bands or artists whose legacies have lasted decades (for example Colosseum, the Moody Blues, or 10cc). Some progressive rock bands and artists do, however, combine their earlier repertoires with newer and current material, examples being King Crimson, Peter Gabriel, David Gilmour, and Steven Wilson. Given that this book was written between 2016 and 2017 and the interviews were also carried out during that time period, it is worth a brief examination of how other works on progressive rock from earlier periods have been concluded.

Edward Macan's final statements in *Rocking the Classics* predict a progressive rock future in which only long-established bands will be performing in the genre. He maintains that during the 1990s, King Crimson were in a process of "self-quotation," a statement that does not fit what the band's members have stated in interviews for this book.[3] Also, though Macan's prediction of well-established bands becoming "cultural, musical and business institutions" may be partially true in some commercially successful cases, his statement about these bands being popular only among "an aging taste public" is, again, incorrect given statements made by current performers.[4] Moreover, he states that in order to maintain status, existing progressive rock will always have to make adjustments to the progressive rock of the 1970s. This is erroneous and cannot be used as a description of the newer bands discussed in this book. Macan's book, written in 1997, when several of the bands discussed were already achieving success, is ambiguous in its final paragraph in which Macan says that there will be only a small fan base for the music but that the music will be self-perpetuating and avoid musical stagnation because fans "refuse to countenance the introduction of any influences outside of the 'classic' Yes/Genesis/ELP [Emerson, Lake and Palmer] lineage into the neo-progressive [Macan's term for post-1970s progressive rock] style."[5] Again, he does not acknowledge what had already been happening successfully since the 1980s.

Paul Stump is highly critical of Macan's nostalgic views and in his own revised work, published in 2010, he states that even Rick Wakeman is dismissive of Yes' 2005 recording *Union*, referring to it as "Onion" because when he hears it, it brings tears to his eyes.[6] Despite Wakeman's statement coming from a more recent edition of Stump's original 1997 study of progressive rock, Stump mostly remains tied to descriptions of long-established progressive bands' and those performers' current activities, while proposing that a "new" band such as Radiohead is now part of what might be termed "the establishment." In doing so, he does not discuss many contemporary progressive bands and artists, instead including many alternative, indie, and experimental bands, some of which may be regarded as on the fringes of progressive rock, though not many. Stump does, however, come close to explaining what contemporary progressive rock might have become when he points out that Allan F. Moore believes that "taking liberties with the exigencies of the printed score in effect removes the boundaries between different musics."[7] For Stump, this removal "provides endless possibilities for textural play," an apt description of progressive rock in any of its stages.[8] Stump does point out, however, that Macan and Bill Martin provide "exhilarating writings on the genre [that] leave nobody in any doubt as to the depth to which progressive roots were laid down in the minds of thinking and cosmopolitan young Americans."[9]

This view is significant in the development of progressive rock in the United States, given its roots in middle-class U.K. youth, initially spreading to Europe before the United States. It also ties in with the fusions of jazz and rock by John McLaughlin, Chick Corea, and Josef Zawinul, respectively English, American, and German, all of whom combined styles from other areas of music and all of whom were members of U.S. bands that influenced some of the interviewees for this book. Moreover, Stump demonstrates his personal preference for earlier progressive rock in his revised edition of his 1997 work. For Stump, genres such as progressive metal need to be reclassified on their own. Although he points out Opeth's "staggering dexterity," he maintains that there is "little commitment to its delivery," and he admits that many more recent progressive rock fans will find this and his other current views to be heretical.[10]

In their concluding chapter, Hegarty and Halliwell are critical of Macan's prediction that progressive rock of the post-1970 period was a "pale shadow" of what preceded it. Macan's view is shared by Bill Wilson and Paul Stump, and each of the three authors seem tied to what Halliwell and Hegarty regard as nostalgia, which they see as an erroneous view of "a slow rise and a terminal fall from which the only return is nostalgia for an ever receding past."[11] Their view, however, that the music industry often absorbs new musical styles that create predictable sounds that lack the organic development apparent in early progressive rock is correct, although they do not acknowledge how many progressive artists and bands have an enduring popularity that has lasted into the new millennium.[12] Significantly, their assumption that progressive rock was not popular between 1976 and 1997 is highly questionable, given the evidence gathered for this book. That said, their concluding statement that progressive rock can be both the past returning with the older bands as well as a progressive rock future "that will only be seen in hindsight" is exactly what has been happening in recent years.[13]

Whereas nostalgia always seems to be apparent among certain sections of the progressive rock audience as described by some of the authors discussed, another concept that has become more evident in contemporary progressive rock is the inclusion of improvisation and a break away from static arrangements. This, again, comes from a significant progressive trope, virtuosity. Rick Wakeman described his first period in Yes as an episode in which every part of the band's performance was prearranged.[14] Wakeman's later performances with the band demonstrated his ability to improvise within Yes' strict musical forms, as demonstrated on *Yessongs* (1973). As King Crimson entered the 1980s, Tony Levin described a more contemporary view among band members that arguably came from the United States, in which members of progressive bands who were influenced by or had performed with Miles Davis, Chick Corea, Josef Zawinul, and Herbie Hancock started to experiment with musical structures in rock and break away from the almost classical music–like restrictions on the printed score.[15] Robin Lumley provides an anecdote about Josef Zawinul's approach to experimentation that is worth noting, as it goes some way in explaining Zawinul's personal approach to improvisation:

> After the gig at the Antibes Jazz Festival in 1977, the whole touring ensemble (Brand X, Weather Report, and the Stanley Clarke Band) were on their way in a coach to the Montreux Jazz Festival for the next gig. I didn't know Joe at all but needless to say, I had *all* his albums! Joe asked me if I'd like to sit next to him! (Wayne Shorter was amazed; 'he never does things like that!'). It turns out that Joe really rated me as a nascent up-and-coming player and went on to give me advice, all across the Alps. He asked me if I was right- or left-handed . . . then he told me to learn to write with the *other* hand, starting now and never failing. This was because writing with the other hand joins up all the lazy neurons in the hand and fingers enabling you, with time, to double your manual dexterity . . . become like *him* . . . in order to play two different keyboards at once with two hands. This I did . . . although I can't claim anything like Joe in technique, but it made a world of difference![16]

Freedom in improvisation in progressive rock is still a question of what an individual songwriter requires of band members. Although Robert Fripp has given more recent (since the mid-1990s) King Crimson musicians extra room to express themselves (hence Jakszyk's comment that no Crimson performance is the same), another songwriter, Steven Wilson, is able to express exactly what he requires from his musicians on each recording he makes. His performances also reflect this, although, like King Crimson, the caliber of musicianship in his band means that any soloist has a great deal of freedom, albeit a structured freedom. Keyboardist Adam Holzman, drummer Marco Minnemann, and guitarists Guthrie Govan and David Kilminster are fine examples of this musical skill. The same approach to performance applies to musicians on Wilson's earlier Porcupine Tree albums.

The fact that some progressive musicians are able to leave a band, perform with other musicians for a number of years, and then reunite raises another issue. The type of band membership fluidity for progressive rock that was evident in the 1970s still exists. As Clem Clempson put it in regard to Colosseum, "we had a great evening [jamming at a member's birthday party] and joked about getting back together" and ultimately "the scale of the demand was quite overwhelming; the combination of that demand from all over Europe and the incredible passion that we encountered from the fans who'd been waiting many years to see us play again" supports this, although the band had to play what the audience expected to hear.[17] It is noticeable on the YouTube recording of one of the early reunion concerts that the audience contains a cross section of age groups. Clempson's statement describes an almost similar reason that the Moody Blues came out of retirement in 1992: for the enjoyment of playing and with mostly original members. They continued performing with symphony orchestras worldwide until 2016, though this band also has to perform a preexisting repertoire.

King Crimson makes only a few references to its past. Jakszyk explained how Fripp chose him and a King Crimson member from the 1970s to enable the band to do this: "I mean I think that was part of what appealed to him about using Mel [Collins, a saxophonist who was in earlier lineups] and maybe me as a singer was that he felt that we could access some of the older material that hasn't been played in decades and in some cases ever."[18]

He also described how the band was preparing for its 2017 world tour and the musical freedom that the current lineup enjoyed:

> We have areas of [improvisation]; there's a number of tunes that we played . . . where we played the beginning and we played the end and we don't really know what's going to happen in the middle. . . . There's a few of those; I'm not sure there's as many as there was before. We currently do two or three and I don't know whether that's because it's such a large lineup. It's an unwieldy thing to do that with. But yes, I mean there's sections and everything where you can move out. In terms of real freedom, I think . . . it's about three or four tunes where, you know, it's different, it's all different every night. And then plus what he's [Robert] done with this group, he's built up a repertoire . . . and we're adding to it for this tour. We start rehearsals in April [2017]. And by the end of that, we will have a repertoire of somewhere in the regions of three and a half hours and we do a different set every night.[19]

From these statements, components that have provided progressive rock with longevity seem to be musical virtuosity and dedication to musical experimentation that lead to a skill-based combination of being able to refer to the genre's past while breaking new ground in its future. Another component is the flexibility of membership of progressive bands.

Given the comments made by Jakszyk, O'Toole, Lumley, and Beggs, membership flexibility thus remains a central progressive rock component, alongside versatility and dedication in musicianship and other musical skills. Moreover, there exists among these musicians a preparedness for any musical challenge that may arise, which may bring about membership change, and this preparedness often leads to session work, composition for oneself, or composition commissions for others, as well as production work. The contemporary progressive rock musician has, therefore, an extremely varied and broad-based skill set that was sometimes apparent in the initial phase of the genre, although perhaps not to such a great extent. A possible reason is that the technologies described by these interviewees were not available in the 1970s. Whereas several bands mentioned have had a stable membership for many years, others have had a kind of "revolving door" that has enabled an even greater sharing of influences and ideas. Going back as far as 1970, this process was responsible for the formation of Emerson (from the Nice), Lake (from the first King Crimson), and Palmer (from Atomic Rooster). Several prominent progressive rock musicians joined some of the most established bands in the genre and were able to be in more than one at any given time or in new bands that evolved from several others. One such musician was bassist and vocalist John Wetton and another is Fairport Convention bassist Dave Pegg, who was simultaneously in both Fairport Convention and Jethro Tull (recording *Crest of a Knave* [1987] and performing with both Fairport and Jethro Tull on the tour that promoted the album). The list goes on with Greg Lake recording with the Who, Rick Wakeman recording with David Bowie on several albums, and in the present with the musical exchanges described by Steven Wilson between himself and Mikael Åkerfeldt and Misha Manoor of Periphery with Animals As Leaders.

In the 1960s and 1970s, pop rock bands whose membership was unstable were likely to lose record contracts. Progressive musical exchanges caused by membership changes actually provided record companies with marketing opportunities brought about by intentional changes in bands' musical directions (Yes' Bill Bruford moving to King Crimson in 1972, for example).

Now flexibility is apparent in contemporary progressive rock. Bassist Nick Beggs, who tours and records with both Steven Wilson and Steve Hackett, also has his own band, the Mute Gods, and is able to combine working in all three bands. He is also an in-demand session musician. Gary O'Toole is also a session musician and, apart from touring with Steve Hackett at the time of this writing, he has performed and recorded for other musicians. He has several plans of his own that maximize his time, which he described as follows:

> I have my studio at home, from which I am starting my online drum lessons, and it will be a resource of material for my students. I have recorded over 150 clips, individual aspects of playing to help them focus their practice. I also have my school in Denmark Street in London, but that may very soon have to move, so another challenge! I did Nad Sylvan's [Steve Hackett's vocalist] album, and a track for Nick Beggs's Mute Gods album, which is great, but my studio is much better equipped now, so I can do much better stuff. A variety of work must be garnered this year, and I am very confident in the business plan I have to make it all work. The *Genesis Revisited 2* album had all but two of the drum tracks recorded at my home studio. Roger [King], the keyboard player, cowriter with Steve on many solo project songs, a producer, and engineer, brought over a computer and hired a load of mics.
>
> I am going to write that [my own] album too! I have been playing guitar for enough years to be able to spell out chord-wise what I want from a band and own a piano and a bass.[20]

Beggs's third band, the Mute Gods, was formed as the result of a conversation between Beggs and the head of A and R (an artist and repertoire executive who looks for new bands) from InsideOut Records, Thomas Weber. Weber's view was that, given Beggs's activities for so many other people, why was he not performing his own music in his own band? When Beggs commented that he needed a market, Weber replied that there was one, so Beggs recorded an album, *Do Nothing till You Hear from Me*, released in 2016, that did "comparatively well."[21] The other two members in the band are Marco Minnemann from Steven Wilson's band on drums and guitar, and Roger King from Steve

Hackett's band who plays keyboards and is the band's producer. The album reached number six in the U.K. Rock and Metal charts and earned a Vanguard Award at the 2016 Progressive Music Awards. The band's second album, *Tardigrades Will Inherit the Earth*, was released early in 2017. Beggs realistically pointed out that most niche musics have their own awards, and he and his band have won progressive awards, although he stated that he does not have Wilson's issues with that and he regards the Mute Gods as "having aspects of progressive rock but being more pop than anything else." When asked about the pressure of being in three bands at once, two of which are continually touring, and writing material for his own band, Beggs's response was that he always has a computer and a soundcard that enable him to compose and record new ideas, not just for himself but for others as well, hence the dedication component mentioned above.

Although this study of progressive rock aims to be an introduction to the genre and to provide a listening guide with explanatory background information, there remains the contentious issue of how it is defined. It is, perhaps, impossible to define with a single word because it means so many different things to so many different composers, performers, and members of its audience. There are, however, several other components that must be apparent in the style, or at least some of them must be present for the progressive descriptor to be used. Musical training is yet another. From the small sample of interviewees for this work, most were musically trained either formally, in family situations in which family members passed on musical skills, or through "on the job" and finding a passion and a talent for what became known as "progressive rock." All of these musicians, and many others like them, honed performance skills that were often criticized in later years as youth culture changed. But they outlasted that particular cultural change as an earlier audience remained and a new one emerged as the progressive genre continued to progress and change—rock music with stylistic progression is therefore perhaps a more apt, but longer, description.

A further component mentioned throughout this work, musical virtuosity, can be a result of both training or individual dedication to one's instrument (most often both). Many progressive musicians were those who had had varying degrees of musical training either at school or, as stated, were members of musical families. It is significant, however, that these musicians developed musical skills during the years following the 1944 Education Act, given that many of the first wave of successful progressive rock musicians were born in the late 1940s or early 1950s. Those fortunate enough to attend liberal arts–oriented schools would have studied music as a required subject. Whether they enjoyed that kind of teaching is, however, another issue! Nevertheless, as many interviewees stated, being open to new ideas and various musical styles was a key factor in their move toward a more virtuosic form of rock music and a move away from much of the pop music of the time (despite several progressive musicians being active session musicians and many playing on the pop recordings of the time).

As Howard Goodall states in his television program, a mid-1960s collision between classical music and popular music opened the way for many experiments between the two genres, particularly in the aforementioned cases of Procol Harum and the Nice, both bands having had classically oriented hits on singles and LPs from 1967 on.[22] The combination of classical orchestral sensibilities with rock music arguably starts with the Moody Blues' collaboration with the London Festival Orchestra and arranger Peter Knight for the album *Days of Future Passed* (1967). Though the album was released five months after *Sgt. Pepper*, its use of orchestration is closer to the expectations of classically oriented fans and was thus easier for them to associate with preexisting tastes than producer George Martin's unusual orchestrations on songs such as "A Day in the Life" or "I Am the Walrus," Beatles songs that are just two examples of their experimental output. It should be noted, however, that Beatles recordings had often featured standard orchestration, the string section on "Eleanor Rigby" (1966) being an example. The lushness of Peter Knight's arrangements for the Moody Blues was a further obvious influence on bands who were to follow both the Moody Blues and the Beatles in the "progressive" move to combine both classical and rock styles, preempting other more varied stylistic combinations that were to follow. As many interviewees for this work point out, their initial experience of music was in learning an instrument that often did not remain their principal instrument but instead led them to experiment with other instruments, which in turn led them to listen to other musical styles. It is this combination of curiosity and open-mindedness that provided a musical eclecticism that drove George Harrison toward Indian classical music, through to the jazz-rock of bands on both sides of the Atlantic culminating, arguably, with Animals As Leaders and their combination of elements taken from jazz, metal, melodic, and softer rock, and even the classicality of the nylon-strung six-string guitar. Robin Lumley puts his views of rock progression as follows:

> All those bands which you quote (like Crimson) who don't need to be replicas of the 1970s . . . one way they do it (as you say) is to write in irregular time signatures, they improvise, they try to push the envelope with original harmonic modes and mind-bending intervals . . . all being "progressive" like the imagination pushes their mind. All very listenable and, if you've got the patience . . . you'll find it very worthwhile. . . . It's like Stravinksy did 100+ years ago taken to steps beyond.[23]

If one follows Lumley's statement, the term "rock progression" may be used perhaps because these musicians always maintained a sense of curiosity of what rock music could become, with what it could be amalgamated, and what it needed to be to retain an audience. Simon Nicol describes Fairport Convention's performances at the annual Cropredy Festival as being able to attract four generations among the band's audiences.[24] Fairport Convention continues to tour and release albums and has had the same lineup since 1996. Moreover, their songwriting members have the curiosity to research historical events from which to create "new" folk songs, thus providing a future legacy of folk music through the vehicle of folk-rock. King Crimson, on the other hand, has certain members who remain mainstays of the band, while leader Robert Fripp's musical curiosity drives his experiments with different combinations of musicians who bring different concepts to the band. Nevertheless, despite a few relatively short breaks, the band still attracts large audiences and regularly embarks on world tours. Curiosity, described by Steven Wilson as one of his main reasons for seeking new areas in which to compose, is thus an extremely important component of the progressive music tropes.

There is also the technological component. As described in chapters 1 and 2, record companies of the late 1960s and early 1970s were financially stable and aware of the student audience that had come of record (LP) buying age at the time. They were therefore prepared to allow bands of the time to experiment mixing rock music with other genres. This experimentation has been well described in interviews for this book. As previously stated, some existing major record labels even formed minor labels dedicated to the genre and to any other music regarded as too experimental for the pop charts. In the new millennium, in which many record companies have ceased to exist or have been taken over by larger record companies, there are many other ways for musicians performing in any style to distribute their music to their audiences. Some still opt for major companies, as the offer of all the business aspects being taken over is an attractive prospect to musicians who wish to concentrate on curiosity-driven creativity. There are the options of streaming and downloading, although musicians still need to work through companies that provide the internet services and collect royalties (a service much like that provided by a record company and a publisher), or selling music in CD or vinyl formats at as many performances as possible, which may be a key to eventual success if a band or artist's music is too obscure or experimental to reach a "progressive" or "rock" mainstream in which commerciality may be a significant factor. On the other hand, there are, at the time of this writing, several smaller record labels that focus on progressive rock that may be found in the Suggested Listening list.

Discussions that concern musical training, possible resultant virtuosity, musical curiosity that involves technology as much as it does performance, eclecticism, experimentation, and the involvement of styles that are not associated with familiar notions of rock music's identity can all become components of modern or contemporary progressive rock. Add to these components an ongoing willingness of musicians to collaborate with a broad selection of other musicians of differing styles, and ultimately there will be further possible descriptors for the style. This possibility indicates that, despite some or all of these elements being present in what we can arguably call "progressive," or even rock music that "progresses," there emerge possible reasons for the causes of some of the issues that alienated it in the mid-1970s and why there is a new and vibrant combination, or fusion, of rock with other musical styles that is currently "progressive" and that is popular with a multi-age audience.

Finally, I have used the term "classical music" throughout this work though it does not do the music justice. As with many other forms of music, using one term is limiting, but most audiences do know what is meant by the word "classical," despite it being merely one period among many others, all of which had their own stages of development and change. There are several other periods that span centuries. Likewise, there are periodic phases in the development of jazz, but "jazz" is always the umbrella term used. In the case of rock music, the number of styles covered have continued to multiply since rock and roll became popular in the 1950s, yet its 1940s predecessors are rarely mentioned in the history of rock music. As Howard Goodall states at the beginning of this chapter, the 1960s seemed to be a "melting pot" of popular music styles that affected the popular music styles that were to follow in later decades, progressive rock being one of them. Some styles lasted, leaving a rich musical legacy; others were what might be called "fads" and were soon forgotten. The legacy of progressive rock, or whatever one wishes to call it, continues because of the components contained within the styles listed. However, although "progressive" suits some people as a descriptor, including myself, it is ultimately up to the composers and musicians who make the music, as well as the audiences listening to it, to call it whatever they want.

To summarize, does a name matter if the music is experimental, virtuosic, creative, exciting, and continually evolving—in other words, progressing and not rooted in nostalgia?

NOTES

INTRODUCTION

1. Chou Wen-chung, "Open Rather Than Bounded," *Perspectives of New Music* 5, no. 1 (Autumn–Winter 1966): 1–6.

2. Terry Pack, interview with author, 18 December 2016.

3. Paul Stump, *The Music's All That Matters—A History of Progressive Rock* (London: Quartet, 1997; rev. ed., Essex: Harbour Books, 2010); Edward Macan, *Rocking the Classics—English Progressive Rock and the Counterculture* (New York: Oxford University Press, 1997); Bill Wilson, *Listening to the Future: The Time of Progressive Rock, 1968–1978* (Chicago: Open Court Publishing, 1998); Paul Hegarty and Martin Halliwell, *Beyond and Before: Progressive Rock since the 1960s* (New York: Continuum International Publishing, 2011).

4. Ian Macdonald, *Revolution in the Head* (London: Fourth Estate, 1994).

5. Allan F. Moore, "Progressive Rock," *The New Grove Dictionary of Music and Musicians*, ed. Stanley Sadie, 2nd ed. (London: Macmillan, 2001), 402.

6. Simon Nicol, interview with author, 16 August 2005.

7. Moore, "Progressive Rock," 402.

8. Deena Weinstein, *Heavy Metal: The Music and Its Culture* (Boston: Da Capo Press, 1991); Robert Walser, *Running with the Devil: Power, Gender and Madness in Heavy Metal Music* (Middleton, CT: Wesleyan University Press, 1993).

9. Clem Clempson, interviews with author, 15 December 2016 and 27 February 2017.

10. John Knightsbridge, interviews with author, 27 January 2016 and 28 February 2017.

11. Nick Beggs, interviews with author, 26 January and 16 October 2016.

12. Beggs, interview with author, January 2016.

13. Gary O'Toole, interviews with author, 26 January and 30 July 2016.

14. O'Toole, interview with author, 26 January 2016.

15. O'Toole, interviews with author, 26 January and 30 July 2016.

16. Rick Fenn, interviews with author, 15 June 2016 and 22 February 2017.

17. Paul Burgess, interview with author, 29 July 2016.

18. Tony Levin, interview with author, 6 September 2016.

19. Levin, interview with author, 6 September 2016.

20. Jakko Jakszyk, interviews with author, 28 September 2016 and 7 February 2017.

21. Jakszyk, interview with author, 28 September 2016.

22. Jakszyk, interview with author, 28 September 2016.

23. Steven Wilson, interview with author, 16 October 2016.

24. Robin Lumley, interview with author, 8 May 2017.

25. Lumley, interview with author, 8 May 2017.

I. "FROM THE BEGINNING"

1. Frank Zappa, television interview, 1984, www.youtube.com/watch?v=Eln3J6BxWN0, (accessed 11 April 2017).

2. Gentle Giant, *Acquiring the Taste*, Vertigo Records, 1971.

3. Jay Keister and Jeremy L Smith, "Musical Ambition, Cultural Accreditation and the Nasty Side of Progressive Rock," *Popular Music* 27, no. 3 (October 2008): 434.

4. For a discussion about the early years of progressive rock as folk-rock and its audience, see Robert G. H. Burns, *Transforming Folk: Innovation and Tradition in English Folk-Rock Music* (Manchester, UK: Manchester University Press, 2012), 118–19.

5. Robin Lumley, interview with author, 8 May 2017.

6. Zoot Money, conversations with author between 1981 and 1986.

7. Allan F. Moore, "Authenticity As Authentication," *Popular Music* 21, no. 2 (2002): 215.

8. Paul Stump, *The Music's All That Matters—A History of Progressive Rock* (London: Quartet, 1997; rev. ed., Essex: Harbour Books, 2010), 148.

9. Charlie Gillett, *The Sound of the City* (London: Souvenir Press, 1983), 401–13.

10. Edward Macan, *Rocking the Classics—English Progressive Rock and the Counterculture.* (New York: Oxford University Press, 1997), 46.

11. Macan, *Rocking the Classics*, 15–21; Richie Unterberger, *Eight Miles High: Folk-Rock's Flight from Haight-Ashbury to Woodstock* (San Francisco: Backbeat Books, 2003), 11–38.

12. Macan, *Rocking the Classics*, 46.

13. John R. Palmer, "Yes 'Awaken,' and the Progressive Rock Style," *Popular Music* 20, no. 2 (2001): 243.

14. Macan, *Rocking the Classics*, 11.

15. For further information on this phenomenon, see Robert G. H. Burns, "British Folk Song of the Great War: Then and Now," *Journal of Military History (Centennial Edition)* 79, no. 4 (October 2015): 1054–77.

16. Michael James Keenan interview in Stump, *The Music's All That Matters*, 332.

17. Colosseum, "Valentyne Suite Three: The Grass Is Greener," *Live Cologne 1994*, www.youtube.com/watch?v=B-htnqmlgKE (accessed 26 April 2017).

18. In terms of musical education, it is worth noting that members of Dream Theater attended Berklee College of Music in Boston.

19. Jon Anderson on Yes: http://yesworld.com/2012/12/jon-anderson-talks-yes-close-to-the-edge-track-by-track (accessed 6 February 2016).

20. Robert Christgau on ELP: www.robertchristgau.com/get_artist.php?name=emerson+lake+and+palmer (accessed 23 February 2016).

21. John Peel on ELP: www.bbc.co.uk/music/reviews/9bvr (accessed 23 February 2016).

22. Stump, *The Music's All That Matters*, 318.

23. *Malleus Maleficarum*: www.malleusmaleficarum.org/introduction-to-online-edition-continued (accessed 9 March 2016).

2. CONCEPTUALITY

1. In the early years of recording reproduction and distribution, there were various disc sizes, including ten-inch discs. There were also various speeds used before the twelve-inch shellac disc, which rotated at 78 rpm, became the industry standard, although other materials had been used in the development process. Once CBS introduced "microgroove," a smaller grooved record requiring a finer stylus in the 1960s, more recording time could be contained on seven-inch singles and long-playing twelve-inch records. Bob Dylan's "Like a Rolling Stone" became the first hit single that lasted around six minutes. It also enabled the introduction of the EP single, which could contain up to four short pop songs.

2. Michael Chanan, *Repeated Takes: A Short History of Recording and Its Effects on Music* (London: Verso, 1995), 45–47.

3. Chanan, *Repeated Takes*, 95–97.

4. One of my first bands in the 1970s had a forty-minute song with no improvisation. We opened our set with this song while on tour supporting Soft Machine, Greenslade (formed by members of Colosseum), and Caravan.

5. Chris Welch, *Melody Maker*, January 1974.

6. Chanan, *Repeated Takes*, 142–43.

7. The statement about songwriting may not apply to *Let It Be*, an album recorded in 1969 before the actual final album, *Abbey Road*, also recorded in 1969. *Let It Be* was released in 1970 and was purposely a return to the Beatles' earlier influences and songwriting styles and to their roots in rock and roll and rhythm and blues.

8. Ian MacDonald, *Revolution in the Head* (London: Fourth Estate, 1994), 180.

9. Graeme Thomson, *George Harrison: Behind the Locked Door* (London: Omnibus Press, 2013), 131–66; Tim Riley, *The Man, the Myth and the Music: Lennon, the Definitive Life* (London: Random House, 2011), 405–13.

10. Riley, *The Man*, 409.

11. Riley, *The Man*, 411.

12. Kari Kallioniemi, *Englishness, Pop and Post-War Britain* (Chicago: Intellect, University of Chicago Press, 2016), 109.

13. Kallioniemi, *Englishness*, 126.

14. Kallioniemi, *Englishness*, 126.

15. Pete Townshend, *Who I Am* (London: HarperCollins, 2012), 64.

16. Townshend, *Who I Am*, 130–33.

17. Townshend, *Who I Am*, 156.

18. Townshend, *Who I Am*, 156–57.

19. Townshend calls it a "song cycle." Townshend, *Who I Am*, 164.

20. Townshend, *Who I Am*, 162.

21. Townshend, conversation with author, February 1979.

22. R. G. H. Burns, *Transforming Folk: Innovation and Tradition in English Folk-Rock Music* (Manchester, UK: Manchester University Press, 2012), 104.

23. Britta Sweers, *Electric Folk* (Oxford: Oxford University Press, 2005), 38–39.

24. Mike Holgate and Ian Waugh, *The Man They Could Not Hang: The True Story of John Lee* (London: History Press, 2013).

25. "Watcher in the Skies" was also released as a single using both sides of the 7-inch single.

26. For a discussion on Gabriel's role in Genesis and his subsequent career, see *Peter Gabriel: From Genesis to Growing Up*, ed. Michael Drewett, Sarah Hill, and Kim Kärki (Farnham, UK: Ashgate, 2010).

27. Paul Hegarty and Martin Halliwell, *Beyond and Before: Progressive Rock since the 1960s* (New York: Continuum International Publishing, 2011), 96.

28. Email correspondence with author, 25 April 2016. Glasser has been an audio engineer since 1975, first in radio and then on National Public Radio in Washington, D.C., where he worked on many projects, including the daily news programs, radio documentaries, concert recording and postproduction, and live concert remote broadcasts. He started a mastering company in 1990 and built his own well-equipped mastering studio in the early 1990s. Glasser won the first of two Grammys in 1997.

29. Email correspondence with author, 25 April 2016.

30. Chanan, *Repeated Takes*, 144. It is worth noting that early Tamla Motown recordings were recorded on three-track machines, although the company's recording engineers had developed an eight-track recording machine three years before Ampex produced their own eight-track recorder. Jon Fitzgerald, "Motown Crossover Hits 1963–66 and the Creative Process," *Popular Music* 14 no. 1 (1995): 1–11; interview with author, 16 May 2016. Les Paul also had successfully linked a number of two-track recorders to make multitrack recordings during the 1950s.

31. Thomson, *George Harrison*, 105–7; www.beatlesbible.com/1966/08/29/candlestick-park-san-francisco-final-concert (accessed 24 April 2016).

32. Emerson, Lake and Palmer also formed a record company called Manticore Records in 1973.

33. Townshend, *Who I Am*, 186–88.

34. Mike Dewe, *The Skiffle Craze* (Aberystwyth, UK: Planet, 1998), 163.

3. ENEMIES AT THE DOOR

1. Conversely, the *Melody Maker* weekly newspaper was read by a broader range of musicians, although this possibly led to the publication's eventual demise.

2. Paul Hegarty and Martin Halliwell, *Beyond and Before: Progressive Rock since the 1960s* (New York: Continuum International Publishing, 2011), 3.

3. U.K. unemployment statistics: http://news.bbc.co.uk/2/hi/uk_news/politics/4553464.stm (accessed 6 May 2016).

4. Sean Albiez, "Know History! John Lydon, Cultural Capital and the Prog/Punk Dialectic," *Popular Music* 22, no. 3 (2003): 305–21.

5. Albiez, "Know History," 361.

6. Eugene Montague, "From Garahge to Garidge: The Appropriation of Garage Rock in the Clash's 'Garageland' (1977)," *Popular Music and Society* 29, no.4 (2006): 427–39, 503. For further discussions on the punk genre, see Dick Hebdige, *Subculture: The Meaning of Style* (London: Richard Clay, 1988), and Jon Savage, *England's Dreaming: Anarchy, Sex Pistols, Punk Rock and Beyond* (London: St. Martin's, 1991).

7. Albiez, "Know History," 358.

8. Rick Fenn, interviews with author, 15 June 2016.

9. Fenn, interview, 2016.

10. Allan F. Moore, "Progressive Rock," *The New Grove Dictionary of Music and Musicians*, ed. Stanley Sadie, 2nd ed. (London: Macmillan, 2001), 402.

11. For a description of the British pub rock scene in the late 1970s and 1980s, see Andrew Bennett, "Going down the Pub! The Pub Rock Scene As a Resource for the Consumption of Popular Music," *Popular Music* 16, no. 1 (January 1997), 97–108.

12. Fenn, interview, 2016.

13. Paul Burgess, interview with author, 29 July 2016.

14. Fenn, interview, 2016.

15. It is worth noting that lead guitars playing harmony were a trademark of another progressive band that were successful earlier than 10cc: Wishbone Ash.

16. Ken Tucker, "Hard Rock on the Rise," in *Rock of Ages: The Rolling Stone History of Rock and Roll*, ed. Geoffrey Stokes Ward and Ken Tucker (New York: Rolling Stone Press, 1986), 484.

17. Journey: www.officialcharts.com/artist/19474/journey (accessed 21 August 2016). For a comprehensive discussion on Rush, see Durrell Bowman, *Experiencing Rush: A Listener's Companion* (Lanham, MD: Rowman & Littlefield, 2015).

18. John Knightsbridge, interviews with author, 27 January 2016.

19. Deena Weinstein, *Heavy Metal: The Music and Its Culture* (Boston: Da Capo Press, 1991), 267.

20. Tucker, "Hard Rock on the Rise," 484.

21. FM radio was developed in the 1930s, but it was not widely used until the 1960s.

22. Weinstein, *Heavy Metal*, 164.

23. Beggs, email, 30 July 2016.

24. Knightsbridge, interview, 2016.

25. For an account of the recording, see Timothy Warner, *Pop Music: Technology and Creativity: Trevor Horn and the Digital Revolution* (Farnham, UK: Ashgate, 2003), 45.

4. A NEW DECADE AND A NEW PROGRESSIVE ROCK

1. Tony Levin, interview with author, 6 September 2016.
2. Levin, interview, 2016.
3. For discussions on the Beat poets, see *The Penguin Book of the Beats*, ed. Ann Charters (London: Penguin Books, 1992).
4. Andrew Sarris, "More Babbitt Than Beatnik," 1967, *New York Times*, www.nytimes.com/books/97/09/07/home/kerouac-paris.html (accessed 4 October 2016).
5. On King Crimson's *Beat*, the song "The Howler" refers to Ginsberg's poem "Howl," which was almost banned upon its 1957 publication (Ann Charters, *The Penguin Book of the Beats* [London: Penguin Books, 1992], xxviii). King Crimson lyrics refer to "the angel of the world's desire placed on trial."
6. Charters, *The Penguin Book of the Beats*, 57.
7. Charters, *The Penguin Book of the Beats*, 9.
8. Charters, *The Penguin Book of the Beats*, 4.
9. Levin, interview, 2016.
10. Robin Lumley, interview with author, 8 May 2017.
11. Lumley, interview, 2017.
12. Steven Wilson, interview with author, 16 October 2016.

5. NEW DIRECTIONS IN THE 1990S AND 2000S

1. Michael Chanan, *Repeated Takes: A Short History of Recording and Its Effects on Music* (New York: Verso, 1995), 153.
2. Chanan, *Repeated Takes*, 153.
3. Email correspondence with author, 25 April 2016.
4. Guide to surround sound: www.dolby.com/us/en/guide/surround-sound-speaker-setup/Fe-1-setup.html (accessed 6 May 2016).
5. Glasser, correspondence, 2016.
6. Steven Wilson, interview with author, 16 October 2016.
7. Wilson, interview, 2016.
8. Jakko Jakszyk, interview with author, 7 February 2017.

9. Richard Cole and Richard Trubo, *Stairway to Heaven: Led Zeppelin Uncensored* (New York: Harper Entertainment, 2002), 198.

10. Cole and Trubo, *Stairway to Heaven*, 198.

11. Wilson, interview, 2016.

12. Paul Hegarty and Martin Halliwell, *Beyond and Before: Progressive Rock since the 1960s* (New York: Continuum International Publishing, 2011), 224.

13. Hegarty and Halliwell, *Beyond and Before*, 223.

14. Paul Stump, *The Music's All That Matters: A History of Progressive Rock* (London: Quartet, 1997; rev. ed., Essex: Harbour Books, 2010), 331.

15. For example, see Oriol Nieto, "Rhythmic and Meter Explorations of a Complex Metal Piece: Meshuggah's Catch 33," http://urinieto.com/wp-content/uploads/2013/08/ RhythmSeminar-Nieto2013.pdf (accessed 20 January 2017); Guy Capuzzo, *A Cyclic Approach to Rhythm and Meter in the Music of Meshuggah*, https://societymusictheory.org/files/2014_handouts/capuzzo.pdf (accessed 20 January 2017); Jonathan Pieslak, "Re-casting Metal: Rhythm and Meter in the Music of Meshuggah," *Music Theory Spectrum* 2, no. 29 (2007): 219–45.

16. Nieto, "Rhythmic and Meter Explorations," 6.

17. Jakszyk, interview, 2017.

18. Adam Holzman, "Optimistic Music in the Age of Fear," www.adamholzman.com (accessed 3 February 2017).

19. Holzman is the son of Elektra Records founder Jac Holzman.

20. Wilson, interview, 2016.

21. Gary O'Toole, interview with author, 30 July 2016.

22. Wilson, interview, 2016.

23. Wilson's band, Porcupine Tree, is well documented by Hegarty and Halliwell, *Beyond and Before*, 272–76 and 285–87.

6. TRIPPING THE LIGHT FANTASTIC

1. Spencer Bright, *Peter Gabriel: An Authorized Biography* (London: Sidwick and Jackson, 1999), 391.

2. Rolling Stone 500 Greatest Albums: www.rollingstone.com/music/lists/500-greatest-albums-of-all-time-20120531/david-bowie-the-rise-and-fall-of-ziggy-stardust-and-the-spiders-from-mars-20120524 (accessed 19 February 2017).

3. Shelton Waldrep, "David Bowie and the Art of Performance," in *Global Glam and Popular Music: Style and Spectacle from the 1970s to the 2000s*, ed. Ian Chapman and Henry Johnson (New York: Routledge, 2016), 43.

4. Peter Gabriel, conversation with author, 1976.

5. Ritchie Blackmore, interview in *Sounds* magazine, 15 December 1979.

6. Deena Weinstein, *Heavy Metal: The Music and Its Culture* (Boston: Da Capo Press, 1991), 288.

7. Allan F. Moore, "Progressive Rock," *The New Grove Dictionary of Music and Musicians*, ed. Stanley Sadie, 2nd ed. (London: Macmillan, 2001), 402.

8. John Willett, *The Theatre of the Weimar Republic* (New York: Holmes and Meier, 1998), 138.

9. Robert Burns, "German Symbolism in Rock Music: National Signification in the Imagery and Songs of Rammstein," *Popular Music* 27, no. 3 (2008): 461.

10. Corrina Kahnke, "Rammstein Rocking the Republic: A Cultural Reading of the Trans/National Shock and Roll Band," in *Rammstein on Fire: New Perspectives on the Music and Performances*, ed. John T. Littlejohn and Michael T. Puttnam (Jefferson, NC: McFarland, 2013), 129.

11. Kahnke, "Rammstein Rocking the Republic," 131; cf. John T. Littlejohn and Michael T. Puttnam, "Rammstein and *Ostalgie*: Longing for Yesteryear," *Popular Music and Society* 33, no. 1 (February 2010): 35–44. *Ostalgie* is a German word made from two words: *Ost* (East) and *Nostalgie* (nostalgia); in other words, a longing for the East German past.

12. Jakko Jakszyk, interview with author, 7 February 2017.

7. NEW LIFE

1. Simon Nicol, interview with author, 16 August 2005; R. G. H. Burns, *Transforming Folk: Innovation and Tradition in English Folk-Rock Music* (Manchester, UK: Manchester University Press, 2012), 52.

2. Nicol, interview, 2005.

3. Burns, *Transforming Folk*, 76–77.

4. Burns, *Transforming Folk*, 52.

5. Clem Clempson, interview with author, 27 February 2017.

6. John Knightsbridge, interview with author, 28 February 2017.

7. Rick Fenn, interview with author, 22 February 2017.

8. Fenn, interview, 2017.

9. Gary O'Toole, interview with author, 30 July 2016.

10. O'Toole, interview, 2016.

11. Jakko Jakszyk, interview with author, 7 February 2017.

12. Jakszyk, interview, 2017.

8. POSTPROG

1. Sales of vinyl recordings: www.theguardian.com/music/2017/jan/03/record-sales-vinyl-hits-25-year-high-and-outstrips-streaming (accessed 8 March 2017).

2. Steven Wilson, interview with author, 16 October 2016.

3. David Glasser: http://forums.stevehoffman.tv/threads/hdtracks-dead-dr.331156 (accessed 8 March 2017).

4. Wilson, interview, 2016.

5. Jakko Jakszyk, interview with author, 7 February 2017.

6. Paul Hegarty and Martin Halliwell, *Beyond and Before: Progressive Rock since the 1960s* (New York: Continuum International Publishing, 2011), 224.

7. Hegarty and Halliwell, *Beyond and Before*, 224 and 237.

8. Hegarty and Halliwell, *Beyond and Before*, 238.

9. Jakszyk, interview, 2017.

10. Jakszyk, interview, 2017.

11. Jakszyk, interview, 2017.

12. *The Tokyo Tapes*, Camino Records, 1998, www.youtube.com/watch?v=L_MSK_zt-nM (accessed 20 March 2017).

9. CONCLUSION

1. Howard Goodall, "Twentieth Century Greats—The Beatles," Channel 4 television, www.youtube.com/watch?v=ZQS91wVdvYc (accessed 20 April 2017).

2. Simon Frith, *Performing Rites* (Oxford: Oxford University Press, 1998), 123–24. On 20 May 2017, Steve Hackett's band performed to a capacity audience at the London Palladium theater (Beggs and O'Toole, correspondence with author, 20 May 2017).

3. Edward Macan, *Rocking the Classics: English Progressive Rock and the Counterculture* (New York: Oxford University Press, 1997), 220.

4. Macan, *Rocking the Classics*, 220.

5. Macan, *Rocking the Classics*, 220.

6. Paul Stump, *The Music's All That Matters: A History of Progressive Rock* (London: Quartet, 1997; rev. ed., Essex: Harbour Books, 2010), 317.

7. Allan F. Moore, *Rock: The Primary Text: Developing a Musicology of Rock* (Aldershot, UK: Ashgate, 1993), 61.

8. Stump, *The Music's All That Matters*, 352.

9. Stump, *The Music's All That Matters*, 326–27.

10. Stump, *The Music's All That Matters*, 331.

11. Hegarty and Halliwell, *Beyond and Before*, 283–84.

12. Hegarty and Halliwell, *Beyond and Before*, 285.

13. Hegarty and Halliwell, *Beyond and Before*, 290.

14. Stump, *The Music's All That Matters*, 353.

15. Moore, *Rock: The Primary Text*, 61.

16. Robin Lumley, interview with author, 8 May 2017. This group of bands, which stylistically hovered between varying degrees of progressive rock and jazz, continued between 1976 and 1978, sometimes with the addition of the Billy Cobham Big Band.

17. Clem Clempson, interview with author, 27 February 2017.

18. Jakko Jakszyk, interview with author, 7 February 2017.

19. Jakszyk, interview, 2017.

20. Gary O'Toole, interview with author, 30 July 2016.

21. Nick Beggs, interview with author, 16 October 2016.

22. The Nice intended the combination of Antonin Dvořák's *Symphony No.9 (From the New World)* and Leonard Bernstein's "America" from *West Side Story* to be a protest against the war in Vietnam.

23. Lumley, interview, 2017.

24. R. G. H. Burns, *Transforming Folk: Innovation and Tradition in English Folk-Rock Music* (Manchester: Manchester University Press, 2012), 203.

SUGGESTED LISTENING

Most of these artists have many more albums in their respective reper-toires. The following list features the names of albums featured in this study or that were performed by the interviewees contributing to it. Thus, this is an objective list and not a subjective one.

ANIMALS AS LEADERS

Animals As Leaders. Prosthetic Records. 2009.
Weightless. Prosthetic Records. 2011.
The Joy of Motion. Sumerian Records. 2014.
The Madness of Many. Sumerian Records. 2016.

THE BEACH BOYS

Pet Sounds. Capitol Records. 1967.

THE BEATLES

Revolver. Parlophone Records. 1966.
Sergeant Pepper's Lonely Hearts Club Band. Parlophone Records. 1967.

The Beatles (The White Album). Apple Records. 1968.
Abbey Road. Apple Records. 1969.
Let It Be. Apple Records. 1970.

BIG BIG TRAIN

The Infant Hercules. Giant Electric Pea. 1993.
English Electric Part 1. GEP Records. 2012.
English Electric Part 2. GEP Records. 2013.

BRAND X

Moroccan Roll. Charisma Records. 1977.
Masques. Charisma Records. 1978.

THE BYRDS

Sweetheart of the Rodeo. CBS Records. 1968.

COLOSSEUM

Those Who Are about to Die. Sanctuary Records. 1969.
Valentyne Suite. Vertigo Records. 1969.
Daughter of Time. Dunhill Records. 1970.
Live Cologne 1994. Angel Air Records. 1994.
Live '05. Ruf Records. 2010.

THE CONTORTIONIST

Clarivoyant. eOne Music/Good Fight Records. 2017.

CREAM

Disraeli Gears. Polydor Records. 1967.
Wheels of Fire. Polydor Records. 1968.

DREAM THEATER

Live at Budokan. Atlantic Records. 2004.

EMERSON, LAKE AND PALMER

Tarkus. Island Records. 1971.
Pictures at an Exhibition. Island Records. 1971.
Trilogy. Atlantic Records. 1972.
Brain Salad Surgery. Manticore Records. 1973.
Black Moon. Victory Records. 1991.

FAIRPORT CONVENTION

Liege and Lief. Island Records. 1969.
Babbacombe Lee. Island Records. 1971.
35th Anniversary Concert. Secret Films DVD. 2002.

GENESIS

Foxtrot. Charisma Records. 1972.
Genesis Live. Charisma Records. 1973.
Selling England by the Pound. Charisma/Atlantic. 1974.
The Lamb Lies Down on Broadway. Charisma Records. 1974.

GENTLE GIANT

Acquiring the Taste. Vertigo Records. 1971.

DAVID GILMOUR

Remember That Night. David Gilmour Music Ltd. DVD/Blu-Ray. 2007.

ILLUSION

Enchanted Caress. Island Records. 1979.

JAKSZYK, FRIPP, AND COLLINS

A Scarcity of Miracles. DGM Records. 2011.

JETHRO TULL

Aqualung. Chrysalis/Island. 1971.
Thick As a Brick. Chrysalis Records. 1972.
Crest of a Knave. Chrysalis Records. 1987.

JIMI HENDRIX

Are You Experienced. Track Records. 1967.

JOHN MAYALL'S BLUESBREAKERS

Bluesbreakers—John Mayall with Eric Clapton. Decca Records. 1966.

JON LORD

Concerto for Rock Group and Orchestra. Deep Purple and the Royal Philharmonic Orchestra. Malcolm Arnold. Harvest Records. 1970.

KING CRIMSON

In the Court of the Crimson King. Island Records. 1969.
Lark's Tongues in Aspic. Island Records. 1973.
Starless and Bible Black. Atlantic Records. 1974.
Discipline. EG/Warner Brothers Records. 1981.
Beat. EG/Warner Brothers Records. 1982.
Three of a Perfect Pair. EG/Warner Brothers Records. 1984.
Thrak. Virgin Records. 1995.
Thrakattak. DGM Records. 1996.
Live at the Orpheum. DGM Records. 2015.
Live in Chicago June 28th. DGM Records. 2017.

THE KINKS

The Kinks Are the Village Green Preservation Society. Pye Records.
1969.
UK Jive. MCA Records. 1989.

LED ZEPPELIN

Houses of the Holy. Atlantic Records. 1973.
Physical Graffiti. Swansong Records. 1975.

MAHAVISHNU ORCHESTRA

The Inner Mounting Flame. CBS/Columbia. 1971.
Birds of Fire. CBS/Columbia. 1973.

MARILLION

Clutching at Straws. EMI Records. 1987.
Fuck Everyone and Run (FEAR). earMusic. 2016.

MESHUGGAH

Catch Thirty-Three. Nuclear Blast Records. 2005.

MILES DAVIS

Bitches Brew. Columbia Records. 1970.

THE MOODY BLUES

Days of Future Passed. Deram Records. 1967.
A Question of Balance. Threshold Records. 1970.

THE MUTE GODS

Do Nothing till You Hear from Me. InsideOut Records. 2016.
Tardigrades Will Inherit the Earth. InsideOut Records. 2017.

PETER GABRIEL

Peter Gabriel. Charisma Records. 1976.
So. Charisma/Geffen. 1986.
Us. Real World Records. 1992.

PINK FLOYD

Piper at the Gates of Dawn. EMI/Columbia. 1967.
A Saucerful of Secrets. EMI/Columbia. 1968.
Ummagumma. Harvest Records. 1969.
Dark Side of the Moon. Harvest Records. 1973.
Wish You Were Here. Harvest Records. 1975.
The Wall. Harvest Records. 1979.
A Momentary Lapse of Reason. EMI/Columbia. 1987.

PORCUPINE TREE

In Absentia. Lava Records. 2002.
Deadwing. Lava Records. 2005.
Fear of a Blank Planet. Atlantic Records. 2007.

RAMMSTEIN

Live aus Berlin. Motor Music. 1999.
Völkerball. Universal Music Group. 2006.

RENAISSANCE

Illusion. Island Records. 1971.

RETURN TO FOREVER

Where Have I Known You Before. Polydor Records. 1974.
No Mystery. Polydor Records. 1975.

RICK WAKEMAN

The Six Wives of Henry VIII. A&M Records. 1973.
Journey to the Center of the Earth. A&M Records. 1974.
The Myths and Legends of King Arthur and the Knights of the Round Table. A&M Records. 1975.

RUSH

Exit . . . Stage Left. Mercury Records. 1981.

THE SMALL FACES

Ogden's Nut Gone Flake. Immediate Records. 1968.

SOFT MACHINE

Bundles. Harvest Records. 1975.
Alive and Well: Recorded in Paris. Harvest Records. 1978.

SPOCK'S BEARD

Brief Nocturnes and Dreamless Sleep. Insideoutmusic/Century Media. 2013.

STEELEYE SPAN

Please to See the King. B and C Records. 1971.
Below the Salt. Chrysalis Records. 1972.
Parcel of Rogues. Chrysalis Records. 1973.

STEVEN WILSON

Grace for Drowning. Kscope Records. 2011.
The Raven That Refused to Sing (and Other Stories). Kscope Records. 2013.
Hand.Cannot.Erase. Kscope Records. 2015.
4½. Kscope Records. 2016.

10CC

The Original Soundtrack. Mercury Records. 1975.
How Dare You! Mercury Records. 1976.
Deceptive Bends. Mercury Records. 1977.

TESSERACT

Polaris. Kscope Records. 2015.

TOOL

Lateralus. Volcano Entertainment. 2001.

VAN DER GRAAF GENERATOR

The Least We Can Do Is Wave to Each Other. Charisma/Probe. 1970.
H to He Who Am the Only One. Charisma/Dunhill. 1970.
Trisector. Virgin/EMI. 2008.

THE WHO

A Quick One (While He's Away). Decca Records. 1966.
Tommy. Decca/MCA. 1969.
Live at Leeds. Decca/MCA. 1970.
Quadrophenia. Track/MCA.1973.

YES

Time and a Word. Atlantic Records. 1970.
The Yes Album. Atlantic Records. 1970.
Fragile. Atlantic Records. 1971.
Tales from Topographic Oceans. Atlantic Records. 1973.
Yessongs. Atlantic Records. 1973.
Drama. Atlantic Records. 1980.

SUGGESTED READING

Albiez, Sean. "Know History! John Lydon, Cultural Capital and the Prog/Punk Dialectic." *Popular Music* 22, no. 3 (November 2003): 305–21.

Anderson, Jon. "Jon Anderson Talks Close to the Edge Track by Track." Accessed 6 February 2016, http:// yesworld.com/2012/12/jon-anderson-talks-yes-close-to-the-edge-track-by-track/.

Baker, Giles. "5.1 Speaker Placement." Accessed 6 May 2016, www.dolby.com/us/en/guide/surround-sound-speaker-setup/5-1-setup.html.

The Beatles Bible. "The Beatles Last Concert at Candlestick Park." Accessed 24 April 2016, www.beatlesbible.com/1966/08/29/candlestick-park-san-francisco-final-concert/.

Bennett, Andrew. "Going Down the Pub! The Pub Rock Scene As a Resource for the Consumption of Popular Music." *Popular Music* 16, no. 1 (January 1997): 97–108.

Bowman, Durrell. *Experiencing Rush: A Listener's Companion*. Lanham, MD: Rowman & Littlefield, 2015.

Bright, Spencer. *Peter Gabriel: An Authorized Biography*. London: Sidwick and Jackson, 1999.

Burns, R. G. H. "German Symbolism in Rock Music: National Signification in the Imagery and Songs of Rammstein." *Popular Music* 27, no. 3 (October 2008): 457–72.

———. *Transforming Folk: Innovation and Tradition in English Folk-Rock Music*. Manchester, UK: Manchester University Press, 2012.

———. "British Folk Song of the Great War: Then and Now." *Journal of Military History (Centennial Edition)* 79, no. 4 (October 2015): 1054–77.

Capuzzo, Guy. "A Cyclic Approach to Rhythm and Meter in the Music of Meshuggah." Accessed 20 June 2017, https://societymusictheory.org/files/2014_handouts/capuzzo.pdf.

Chanan, Michael. *Repeated Takes: A Short History of Recording and Its Effects on Music*. New York: Verso, 1995.

Charters, Ann. *The Penguin Book of the Beats*. London: Penguin Books, 1992.

Christgau, Robert. "Emerson, Lake and Palmer." Accessed 23 February 2016, www.robertchristgau.com/get_artist.php?name=emerson+lake+and+palmer.

Cole, Richard, and Richard Trubo. *Stairway to Heaven: Led Zeppelin Uncensored*. New York: Harper Entertainment, 2002.

Colosseum. "Valentyne Suite Three—The Grass Is Always Greener." *Live Cologne 1994*. Accessed 26 April 2017, www.youtube.com/watch?v=B-htnqmlgKE.

Dewe, Mike. *The Skiffle Craze*. Aberystwyth, UK: Planet, 1998.

Drewett, Michael, Sarah Hill, and Kim Kärki, eds. *Peter Gabriel: From Genesis to Growing Up*. Farnham, UK: Ashgate, 2010.

Ellis-Petersen, Hannah. "Record Sales: Vinyl Hits 25 Year High." *Guardian*. Accessed 8 March 2017, www.theguardian.com/music/2017/jan/03/record-sales-vinyl-hits-25-year-high-and-outstrips-streaming.

Fitzgerald, Jon. "Motown Crossover Hits 1963–66 and the Creative Process." *Popular Music* 14, vol. 1 (January 1995): 1–11.

Frith, Simon. *Performing Rites.* Oxford: Oxford University Press, 1998.

Gillett, Charlie. *The Sound of the City.* London: Souvenir Press, 1983.

Goodall, Howard. "Twentieth-Century Greats—The Beatles." Channel 4 Television. Accessed 20 April 2017, www.youtube.com/watch?v=ZQS91wVdvYc.

Hackett, Steve, Ian McDonald, and John Wetton. "The Tokyo Tapes." Camino Records, 1998. Accessed 20 March 2017, www.youtube.com/watch?v=L_MSK_zt-nM.

Hebdige, Dick. *Subculture: The Meaning of Style.* London: Richard Clay, 1988.

Hegarty, Paul, and Martin Halliwell. *Beyond and Before: Progressive Rock since the 1960s.* New York: Continuum International Publishing, 2011.

Holgate, Mike, and Ian Waugh. *The Man They Could Not Hang: The True Story of John Lee.* London: History Press, 2013.

Holzman, Adam. "Optimistic Music in the Age of Fear." Accessed 3 February 2017, www.adamholzman.com.

Jones, Chris. "Emerson, Lake and Palmer 'From the Beginning' Review." BBC Television. Accessed 23 February 2016, www.bbc.co.uk/music/reviews/9bvr.

Journey. "Official Charts." Accessed 21 August 2016, www.officialcharts.com/artist/19474/journey.

Kahnke, Corrina. "Rammstein Rocking the Republic: A Cultural Reading of the Trans/National Shock and Roll Band." In *Rammstein on Fire: New Perspectives on the Music and Performances*, ed. John T. Littlejohn and Michael T. Puttnam, 129–32. Jefferson, NC: McFarland, 2013.

Kallioniemi, Kari. *Englishness, Pop and Post-War Britain.* Chicago: Intellect, University of Chicago Press, 2016.

Keister, Jay, and Jeremy L. Smith. "Musical Ambition, Cultural Accreditation and the Nasty Side of Progressive Rock." *Popular Music* 27, vol. 3 (October 2008): 433–56.

Kramer, Heinrch, and James Sprenger. "The Malleus Maleficarum." Translated by the Rev. Montague Summers. Accessed 9 March 2016, www.malleusmaleficarum.org/introduction-to-online-edition-continued.

Littlejohn, John T., and Michael T. Puttnam. "Rammstein and *Ostalgie*: Longing for Yesteryear." *Popular Music and Society* 33, no. 1 (February 2010), 35–44.

Macan, Edward. *Rocking the Classics: English Progressive Rock and the Counterculture.* New York: Oxford University Press, 1997.

MacDonald, Ian. *Revolution in the Head.* London: Fourth Estate, 1994.

Martin, Bill. *Music of Yes: Structure and Vision in Progressive Rock.* Chicago: Open Court, 1996.

Montague, Eugene. "From Garahge to Garidge: The Appropriation of Garage Rock in the Clash's 'Garageland' (1977)." *Popular Music and Society* 29, vol. 4 (October 2006), 427–39, 503.

Moore, Allan F. *Rock: The Primary Text: Developing a Musicology of Rock.* Aldershot: Ashgate, 1993.

———. "Progressive Rock." *The New Grove Dictionary of Music and Musicians*, ed. Stanley Sadie. 2nd ed. London: Macmillan, 2001.

———. "Authenticity As Authentication." *Popular Music* 21, vol. 2 (2002): 209–23.

Nieto, Oriol. "Rhythmic and Meter Explorations of a Complex Metal Piece: Meshuggah's Catch 33." Accessed 20 January 2017, http://urinieto.com/wp-content/uploads/2013/08/RhythmSeminar-Nieto2013.pdf.

Orwell, George. *1984.* Accessed 21 August 2016, http://orwell.ru/library/essays/lion.

Palmer, John R. "Yes 'Awaken,' and the Progressive Rock Style." *Popular Music* 20, vol. 2 (2001): 243–61.

Pieslak, Jonathan. "Re-casting Metal: Rhythm and Meter in the Music of Meshuggah." *Music Theory Spectrum* 2, vol. 29 (2007): 219–45.

Riley, Tim. *The Man, the Myth and the Music: Lennon, the Definitive Life*. London: Random House, 2011.

Rolling Stone. "David Bowie and the Rise and Fall of Ziggy Stardust and the Spiders from Mars, No. 35." Accessed 19 February 2017, www.rollingstone.com/music/lists/, 500-greatest-albums-of-all-time-20120531/david-bowie-the-rise-and-fall-of-ziggy-stardust-and-the-spiders-from-mars-20120524.

Sarris, Andrew. "More Babbitt Than Beatnik." 1967. *New York Times*. Accessed 4 October 2016, www.nytimes.com/books/97/09/07/home/kerouac-paris.html.

Savage, Jon. *England's Dreaming: Anarchy, Sex Pistols, Punk Rock and Beyond*. London: St. Martin's, 1991.

Stratton, Jon. "Capitalism and Romantic Ideology in the Record Business." *Popular Music* 3 (1983): 143–56.

Stump, Paul. *The Music's All That Matters: A History of Progressive Rock*. London: Quartet, 1997. Rev. ed., Essex: Harbour Books, 2010.

Sweers, Britta. *Electric Folk*. Oxford: Oxford University Press, 2005.

Thomson, Graeme. *George Harrison: Behind the Locked Door*. London: Omnibus Press, 2013.

Townshend, Pete. *Who I Am*. London: HarperCollins, 2012.

Tucker, Ken. "Hard Rock on the Rise." In *Rock of Ages: The Rolling Stone History of Rock and Roll*, ed. Geoffrey Stokes Ward and Ken Tucker, 480–87. New York: Rolling Stone Press, 1986.

Unterberger, Richie. *Eight Miles High: Folk-Rock's Flight from Haight-Ashbury to Woodstock*. San Francisco: Backbeat Books, 2003.

Waldrep, Shelton. "David Bowie and the Art of Performance." In *Global Glam and Popular Music: Style and Spectacle from the 1970s to the 2000s*, ed. Ian Chapman and Henry Johnson, 42–54. New York: Routledge, 2016.

Walser, Robert. *Running with the Devil: Power, Gender and Madness in Heavy Metal Music*. Middleton, CT: Wesleyan University Press, 1993.

Warner, Timothy. *Pop Music: Technology and Creativity: Trevor Horn and the Digital Revolution*. Farnham, UK: Ashgate, 2003.

Weinstein, Deena. *Heavy Metal: The Music and Its Culture*. Boston: Da Capo Press, 1991.

Willett, John. *The Theatre of the Weimar Republic*. New York: Holmes and Meier, 1998.

Wilson, Bill. *Listening to the Future: The Time of Progressive Rock, 1968–1978*. Chicago: Open Court Publishing, 1998.

Zappa, Frank. Television interview. 1984. Accessed 10 April 2017, www.youtube.com/watch?v=Eln3J6BxWN0.

INDEX

ABOUT THE AUTHOR

Dr. Robert G. H. Burns began his career as a professional musician in the early 1970s and performed as a touring and recording bass guitarist for major American soul artists such as Sam and Dave, Isaac Hayes, the Stylistics, and Edwin Starr. In 1979, he was invited to perform in the rock opera *Tommy* by its composer, Pete Townshend of the Who.

Burns became a "first-call" session bass guitarist in the 1980s and recorded for Jon Lord and Ian Paice of Deep Purple, Donna Summer, Atomic Rooster, Zoot Money and the Big Roll Band, and Vivian Stanshall of the Bonzo Dog Band. He also played on several television and film soundtracks such as *Not the Nine O'Clock News*, *Three of a Kind*, *The Lenny Henry Show*, *Alas Smith and Jones*, *Red Dwarf*, *Blackadder*, *Mr. Bean*, *A Perfect Spy*, *2.4 Children*, and *French and Saunders*.

Live performances and touring continued with jazz trumpeter Ian Carr (biographer of Miles Davis and Keith Jarrett) in Carr's band, Nucleus. Burns performed on three world tours as musical director for Eric Burdon of the Animals between 1981 and 1986, as well as in the musical, *ABBAcadabra*, working for Bjorn Ulvaeus and Benny Anderson of ABBA and lyricists Don Black and Sir Tim Rice.

Between 1989 and 1996, Burns performed with Dave Gilmour (Pink Floyd), James Burton (Elvis Presley), Albert Lee (Emmylou Harris), Clem Clempson (Colosseum), Neil Hubbard (Roxy Music), Snowy White (Thin Lizzy), and Frank Gambale (Chick Corea). He also recorded and toured with Jerry Donahue (Joan Armatrading, Fairport Convention) promoting Jerry's solo album, *Neck of the Wood*. He is currently a member of Subject2Change, a Dunedin-based jazz fusion sextet producing three albums, and the iconic Dunedin band, the Verlaines. Burns has performed on this band's last two albums with a new double-album due for release.

Since 2001, Burns has lectured on a variety of musical subjects at the University of Otago in New Zealand, and he has published extensively on the relationship between rock and folk music as a means of reinforcing national identity. He is currently an associate professor of music in the Department of Music, Theatre, and Performing Arts.